WHILE THE SUN SHINES

A Comedy in Three Acts

by Terence Rattigan

samuelfrench.co.uk

THINKING ABOUT PERFORMING A SHOW?

There are thousands of plays and musicals available to perform from Samuel French right now, and applying for a licence is easier and more affordable than you might think

From classic plays to brand new musicals, from monologues to epic dramas, there are shows for everyone.

Plays and musicals are protected by copyright law, so if you want to perform them, the first thing you'll need is a licence. This simple process helps support the playwright by ensuring they get paid for their work and means that you'll have the documents you need to stage the show in public.

Not all our shows are available to perform all the time, so it's important to check and apply for a licence before you start rehearsals or commit to doing the show.

LEARN MORE & FIND THOUSANDS OF SHOWS

Browse our full range of plays and musicals, and find out more about how to license a show

www.samuelfrench.co.uk/perform

Talk to the friendly experts in our Licensing team for advice on choosing a show and help with licensing

plays@samuelfrench.co.uk   020 7387 9373

 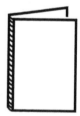

MUSIC USE NOTE

Licensees are solely responsible for obtaining formal written permission from copyright owners to use copyrighted music in the performance of this play and are strongly cautioned to do so. If no such permission is obtained by the licensee, then the licensee must use only original music that the licensee owns and controls. Licensees are solely responsible and liable for all music clearances and shall indemnify the copyright owners of the play(s) and their licensing agent, Samuel French, against any costs, expenses, losses and liabilities arising from the use of music by licensees. Please contact the appropriate music licensing authority in your territory for the rights to any incidental music.

USE OF COPYRIGHT MUSIC

A licence issued by Samuel French Ltd to perform this play does not include permission to use the incidental music specified in this copy.

Where the place of performance is already licensed by the PERFORMING RIGHT SOCIETY (PRS) a return of the music used must be made to them. If the place of performance is not so licensed then application should be made to the PRS, 2 Pancras Square, London, N1C 4AG.

A separate and additional licence from PHONOGRAPHIC PERFORMANCE LTD, 1 Upper James Street, London W1F 9DE (www.ppluk.com) is needed whenever commercial recordings are used.

IMPORTANT BILLING AND CREDIT REQUIREMENTS

If you have obtained performance rights to this title, please refer to your licensing agreement for important billing and credit requirements.

**Other plays by TERENCE RATTIGAN
published and licensed by Samuel French**

Adventure Story

Before Dawn

The Browning Version

Cause Célèbre

The Deep Blue Sea

French without Tears

Harlequinade

In Praise of Love

Man and Boy

Ross

Separate Tables

The Sleeping Prince

A Tale of Two Cities

Variation on a Theme

The Winslow Boy

**Other plays by TERENCE RATTIGAN
licensed by Samuel French**

A Bequest to the Nation

Less than Kind (Love in Idleness)

Who Is Sylvia?

**FIND PERFECT PLAYS TO PERFORM AT
www.samuelfrench.co.uk/perform**

ABOUT THE AUTHOR

(1911–1977)

Born in London on 10 June 1911, Terence Rattigan was educated at Harrow (Scholar) from 1925 to 1930 and Trinity College, Oxford (History Scholarship) BA to 1933. He served as a flight lieutenant in the Central Command, RAF from 1940 to 1945. In 1934 he had become a full-time playwright.

His many successful plays include *French without Tears, After the Dance, Flare Path, Love in Idleness, While the Sun Shines, The Winslow Boy, The Browning Version, Harlequinade, Adventure Story, Who Is Sylvia?, The Deep Blue Sea, The Sleeping Prince, Separate Tables, Variation on a Theme, Ross, Man and Boy, A Bequest to the Nation, In Praise to the Nation, Cause Célèbre.*

Terence Rattigan still holds the record of being the only playwright to have notched more than 1000 performances for two separate plays, namely, *French Without Tears* and *While The Sun Shines.*

During the war years, he had three plays running on Shaftesbury Avenue: *Flare Path* at the Apollo, *While the Sun Shines* at the Globe and *Love in Idleness* at the Lyric.

He wrote screenplays of *French without Tears, The Way to the Stars, Journey Together, While the Sun Shines, The Winslow Boy, The Browning Version, The Prince and The Showgirl, Separate Tables, The Sound Barrier, The Man Who Loved Redheads, The Deep Blue Sea, The Final Test, The VIPs, The Yellow Rolls-Royce, Goodbye Mr Chips, Conduct Unbecoming, A Bequest to the Nation* – and collaborated on *The Quiet Wedding, The Day Will Dawn, English without Tears, Uncensored, Brighton Rock, Bond Street.* His television plays include: *Heart to Heart, Adventure Story, High Summer, After the Dance* was shown in the performance series on BBC 2 in 1993 and *The Deep Blue Sea* was recorded for the same series. In 1958 he was awarded a CBE, and in 1971 he became Knight Bachelor. Sir Terence Rattigan died in 1977.

For further information on Terence Rattigan, visit www.terencerattigan.com.

To join the Terence Rattigan Society, visit www.theterencerattigansociety.co.uk.

ORANGE TREE THEATRE

A powerhouse of independent theatre

The Orange Tree (OT) is an award-winning, independent theatre. Recognised as a powerhouse that creates high-quality productions of new and rediscovered plays, we entertain 70,000 people across the UK every year.

The OT's home in Richmond, South West London, is an intimate theatre with the audience seated all around the stage: watching a performance here is truly a unique experience.

We believe in the power of dramatic stories to entertain, thrill and challenge us; plays that enrich our lives by enhancing our understanding of ourselves and each other.

As a registered charity (266128) sitting at the heart of its community, we work with 10,000 people in Richmond and beyond through participatory theatre projects for people of all ages and abilities.

The Orange Tree Theatre's mission is to enable audiences to experience the next generation of theatre talent, experiment with ground-breaking new drama and explore the plays from the past that inspire the theatre-makers of the present. To find out how you can help us to do that you can visit **orangetreetheatre.co.uk/discover**

ORANGETREETHEATRE.CO.UK
TWITTER @OrangeTreeThtr | FACEBOOK/INSTAGRAM: OrangeTreeTheatre

Development & Communications Assistant **DAVID ANDREWS**
Education Director **IMOGEN BOND**
Technical Manager **STUART BURGESS**
Press & Marketing Director **BEN CLARE**
Education & Participation Assistant **IZZY COTTERILL**
Development Manager **REBECCA FRATER**
Finance Manager **CAROLINE GOODWIN**
Theatre Administrator **LAURA HEPWORTH**
Deputy Technical Manager **LISA HOOD**
Interim Production Technician **RHEA JACQUES**
Development & Communications Director **ALEX JONES**
Literary Associate **GUY JONES**
Artistic Director **PAUL MILLER**
General Manager **SARAH MURRAY**
Executive Director **HANNA STREETER**
Development Manager (maternity cover) **SCOTT TUCKER**
Youth Theatre Programme Director **FREYJA WINTERSON**

This production of *While the Sun Shines* opened at the Orange Tree Theatre, London, on 11 June 2019 with the following cast and creatives:

Lady Elisabeth Randall	Sabrina Bartlett
Horton	John Hudson
The Earl of Harpenden	Philip Labey
The Duke of Ayr & Stirling	Michael Lumsden
Lieutenant Colbert	Jordan Mifsúd
Lieutenant Mulvaney	Julian Moore-Cook
Mabel Crum	Dorothea Myer-Bennett

Director	Paul Miller
Designer	Simon Daw
Lighting Designer	Mark Doubleday
Sound Designer & Composer	Elizabeth Purnell
Voice & Dialect Coach	Emma Woodvine
Casting Consultant	Vicky Richardson

While the Sun Shines was first produced at the Globe Theatre, London, on 24 December 1943, with the following cast of characters:

HORTON	Douglas Jefferies
THE EARL OF HARPENDEN	Michael Wilding
LIEUTENANT MULVANEY	Hugh McDermott
LADY ELIZABETH RANDALL	Jane Baxter
THE DUKE OF AYR AND STIRLING	Ronald Squire
LIEUTENANT COLBERT	Eugene Deckers
MABEL CRUM	Brenda Bruce

The play was directed by Anthony Asquith.

The action passes in the sitting room of Lord Harpenden's chambers in the Albany, London.

ACT I
Morning.

ACT II
Night.

ACT III
Scene One – Late night.
Scene Two – Morning.

ACT I

Scene. The sitting room of **LORD HARPENDEN**'s *chambers in the Albany, London.*

A large, square room, furnished solidly with late eighteenth-century mahogany furniture. Double doors back centre lead into the bedroom; a single door left into the hall. Large windows take up most of the right wall.

A ground plan will be found at the end of the play.

At the rise of the curtain the stage is empty, then **HORTON** *enters left, with a breakfast tray. He is a thin, gloomy-faced man of about fifty. He puts the tray down on a stool left of the settee and knocks gently on the bedroom door. Receiving no reply, he opens the door and, goes in – to emerge instantly. He closes the door again, ponders a second, and then knocks more loudly. There is still no answer. He knocks again. The* **EARL OF HARPENDEN** *comes out, wearing a dressing gown and tying the cord, looking tousled and sleepy. He is a young man of twenty-three or twenty-four, of rather frail appearance.*

HARPENDEN What's the matter?

HORTON Your breakfast is ready, my Lord.

HARPENDEN Yes. So I see. *(moving down left)* But why did you dart in and out like that, like a scared rabbit? *(He surveys his appearance in a wall mirror down left, and gives a faint shudder of disgust. He begins to comb his hair with a small pocket comb, then moves up centre.)* Oh, Horton, bring another breakfast, will you?

HORTON Yes, my Lord.

HARPENDEN What have you got?

HORTON Well, there's some spam.

HARPENDEN No, don't waste the spam, it's far too useful for making sandwiches late at night. *(He crosses and sits on the settee.)* What about sausages?

HORTON *(handing him a newspaper)* I can manage one, my Lord.

HARPENDEN That'll do.

HORTON It's tea and not coffee, isn't it, my Lord?

HARPENDEN What do you mean? *(opening the newspaper)*

HORTON Miss Crum prefers tea to coffee for breakfast.

HARPENDEN Miss Crum? Who said anything about Miss Crum?

HORTON Isn't it Miss Crum?

HARPENDEN No, it is *not* Miss Crum.

HORTON *(doubtfully)* It looked like Miss Crum.

HARPENDEN *(raising his voice)* I don't care who it looked like – it is not Miss Crum. As a matter of fact, it isn't Miss Anybody—

HORTON Mrs Chappel?

HARPENDEN Horton – you haven't by any chance forgotten that I'm getting married tomorrow?

HORTON No, my Lord.

HARPENDEN Very well, then. Now will you kindly go into that room, draw the curtains, take a look round, and then come out and tell me how sorry you are.

HORTON I hardly like to do that, my Lord.

HARPENDEN Go on. *(He motions* HORTON *towards the door.)*

HORTON *exits centre, leaving the door open. The sound of curtains being drawn, and the lights come up.* HORTON *re-appears, closing the doors behind him.*

HORTON I'm extremely sorry, my Lord.

HARPENDEN Thank you, Horton.

HORTON *(crossing down centre)* Funny, it looked just like Miss Crum, the way she sleeps all curled up with her arm over her face— *(Going to the door left)*

HORTON is interrupted by a wail from HARPENDEN, who has taken the cover off his breakfast dish.

HARPENDEN Horton! What's happened to my grandmother's other egg?

HORTON Well, my Lord...

HARPENDEN There were two – you know there were. She sent me two and I had one yesterday – now where's the other?

There is a slight pause before HORTON can gain enough courage to answer. He moves centre.

HORTON There was an accident, my Lord.

HARPENDEN Oh, no!

HORTON I'm afraid so, my Lord.

HARPENDEN *(with a wealth of reproach)* Oh, Horton!

HORTON *(moving towards him, gestures as with an egg)* I had taken it out of the refrigerator, and was just going to break it on the side of the frying pan when...

HARPENDEN Please, Horton, this is too painful. I'd rather not hear any more about it.

The telephone bell starts to ring.

HORTON No, my Lord. I'm very sorry. *(moving to answer the phone)* Hullo...yes, m'lady. *(He lowers the receiver.)* Lady Elizabeth.

HARPENDEN *rises, crosses to the armchair left centre, taking the receiver from HORTON. He sits.*

HARPENDEN Hullo, darling, how are you? Have a good journey?
...Not the whole night? ...Couldn't you get a sleeper?
...Well, surely your father could have fixed it for you through
the Air Ministry... Yes, but I consider coming up to marry
me is work of national importance... How are you? ...Yes, I
know, but apart from that, how are you? ...Good. You didn't
have any trouble about leave? ...When? Wednesday? Well,
that gives us six days...

MULVANEY, *a young American in his late twenties,*
appears at the bedroom door. He has swathed an
eiderdown, round his otherwise naked body.

(*to* MULVANEY) Good morning.

MULVANEY Good morning. (*He stares at* HARPENDEN, *looks*
round the room, blinking in the daylight, then wanders
down right to the window, looking out.)

HARPENDEN (*into the telephone*) No, darling, nobody you
know... Well, not this morning, darling, because I've
got an interview at the Admiralty. Let's meet for lunch.
One o'clock at Prunier's. All right? Good. Where are you
staying? Brown's? ...How did you get in? ...Three weeks ago?
...No, I had a very quiet evening, in bed by ten... All right,
don't believe it...it's true... See you at lunch, then... Goodbye. (*He replaces the receiver. To* MULVANEY) Let me get
you a dressing gown.

He goes into the bedroom.

MULVANEY (*speaking as* HARPENDEN *moves to the bedroom*)
Pardon me – where am I?

HARPENDEN (*bringing out a dressing gown*) You're in my
chambers in Albany.

MULVANEY *drops the eiderdown.*

MULVANEY (*putting the dressing gown on deliberately*) What
are chambers?

HARPENDEN Flat! Apartment.

MULVANEY What's Albany?

HARPENDEN (*picking up the eiderdown*) It's a sort of block of chambers – apartments – off Piccadilly. (*He throws the eiderdown into the bedroom.*)

MULVANEY And, if you'll pardon me again, who are you?

HARPENDEN My name's Harpenden.

MULVANEY Mine's Mulvaney. Glad to know you.

They shake hands.

HARPENDEN How do you do. Do you mind if I start my breakfast ? Yours is on the way. (*He crosses to the settee, sits, and starts breakfast.*)

MULVANEY Go right ahead. (*Crossing down centre*) Was that your bed I slept in? (*He sits in the armchair left centre.*)

HARPENDEN Yes.

MULVANEY Oh. Have I been there since ten last night?

HARPENDEN What? Oh no. You see, I didn't see any point in volunteering the information to one's strictly brought up fiancée that one spent half the night in the Jubilee.

MULVANEY The Jubilee? Now that name seems to pull a plug. Was I there last night?

HARPENDEN Well – you looked in—

MULVANEY (*nodding*) And looked out?

HARPENDEN Shall we say your exit was more involuntary than your entrance.

MULVANEY It's coming back to me. They gave me the bum's rush, didn't they?

HARPENDEN You could put it that way, I suppose. I didn't really see it. One minute you were there, doing a *pas seul* in the centre of the floor, and the next minute you were in the street.

MULVANEY What's a *pas seul?*

HARPENDEN A little dance on your own.

MULVANEY Was that what I was doing?

HARPENDEN That is the charitable view of what you were doing.

MULVANEY What's the uncharitable view?

HARPENDEN Pinching Mrs Warner's behind.

MULVANEY Who's Mrs Warner?

HARPENDEN The proprietress of the Jubilee.

MULVANEY Oh, my aching back! So I'm in the street. What happens then?

HARPENDEN Well, when I left the place, about half an hour later, I tripped over you in the blackout.

MULVANEY Gee, was I lying there unconscious all that time?

HARPENDEN Semi-conscious...

MULVANEY Knocked out, huh?

HARPENDEN No. Passed out.

MULVANEY Say, listen – how could you tell the difference?

HARPENDEN I'd rather not go into that at the moment.

MULVANEY Ok, ok. Only let me tell you, concussion can take some funny forms.

HARPENDEN I doubt if concussion would take the form of breathing gin fumes in my face and calling me Dulcie.

MULVANEY Did I call you Dulcie?

HARPENDEN Amongst other things.

MULVANEY Gosh! How did I come to do that, I wonder?

HARPENDEN Not knowing Dulcie, it's hard for me to say.

MULVANEY She's my girl friend back home.

HARPENDEN So I gathered.

MULVANEY You don't look a bit like her.

HARPENDEN That's too bad.

MULVANEY Well, go on. What happened then?

HARPENDEN You wouldn't tell me where you lived. At least, you gave your address as Eight-five-six, Orinoco Avenue, Elizabeth City, Ohio.

MULVANEY Yeah. That's where I live all right.

HARPENDEN Yes, but it didn't help the immediate problem of finding you a bed.

MULVANEY You could have taken me to Jule's Club or somewhere.

HARPENDEN I thought of that, but not knowing the customs of the American Army, I wasn't sure how they would view the parking on their doorstep at four o'clock in the morning of a very pickled lieutenant, inclined to embrace everyone he saw and call them Dulcie.

MULVANEY (after a moment's thought) It would have been ok.

HARPENDEN I didn't like to risk a court martial.

MULVANEY So you brought me here.

HARPENDEN The porter and I carried you up and put you to bed.

MULVANEY Say, I hope I didn't disgrace you.

HARPENDEN Oh, no. The porters are very discreet. They've been used to putting people to bed for well over a hundred years. Lord Byron lived here.

MULVANEY (interested) Did he now? (He rises and moves centre.) Isn't that something? It is kind of old-world, this place, at that.

HARPENDEN Yes, it is. I like it very much. My family have always lived here.

MULVANEY Do they live here now?

HARPENDEN No, I haven't any family – at least, I'm an orphan.

MULVANEY Tough. Gee, it gives one quite a kick to have slept in the same place where Byron used to sleep in. Did he write any of his poetry here, do you think?

HARPENDEN I expect so.

MULVANEY *(quoting. Standing centre)* So we'll go no more a-roving

So late into the night,

Though the...

How does it go on?

HARPENDEN I'm afraid I don't know. I don't read Bryon.

MULVANEY *(remembering suddenly, and speaking quickly)* Though the heart be still as loving

And the moon be still as bright.

Imagine your not reading Byron. *(He sits on the left arm of the settee.)*

HARPENDEN Imagine.

MULVANEY That's funny, you know.

HARPENDEN *(piqued)* I don't see why it's funny – quite a lot of people don't read Byron.

MULVANEY Yeah. But – hell – you live here.

HORTON *enters with another breakfast tray, goes down left, puts the tray on the stool, and places the stool in front of the armchair left chair.*

HARPENDEN Here's your breakfast.

MULVANEY *(to* **HORTON***)* Take it away, buddy. I couldn't use it.

HORTON *looks at* **HARPENDEN** *in doubt.*

HARPENDEN You'd better try to eat something. It's supposed to be good for – er – concussion.

MULVANEY *(rising and crossing to the chair left centre and sitting)* Ok. I'll try a cup of coffee.

HORTON *pours out coffee.*

Gee, I almost forgot to thank you for being my Good Samaritan.

HARPENDEN Oh, that's all right. I hope you'll do the same for me one day.

MULVANEY I certainly will in the event you ever come to Elizabeth City and get yourself thrown out of Smoky Joe's.

HARPENDEN All right, Horton, you can clear this away now. *(He indicates the breakfast tray.)*

HORTON *moves round behind the armchair, and replaces* **HARPENDEN**'s *stool to the left side of the settee.*

HORTON Very good, my Lord.

MULVANEY *starts, looks at* **HORTON** *and then at* **HARPENDEN,** *as if at a strange animal.*

HARPENDEN You're in the Air Corps, aren't you?

MULVANEY *(still staring at* **HARPENDEN***)* That's right.

HARPENDEN Pilot?

MULVANEY Bombardier.

HARPENDEN Liberators?

MULVANEY Forts.

He continues to scrutinize **HARPENDEN,** *who becomes conscious of his gaze and looks uncomfortable.* **HORTON** *meanwhile has collected* **HARPENDEN**'s *tray.*

HORTON Will you be wearing your uniform, my Lord?

HARPENDEN Yes. My best one. I'm going to the Admiralty.

MULVANEY *puts his coffee cup down with a clatter.*

MULVANEY *(rising and moving to* HORTON*)* You wouldn't fool me, would you?

HORTON *(turning to him, tray in hand)* No, sir.

MULVANEY *(to* HARPENDEN*)* Are you a lord?

HARPENDEN Er – yes.

MULVANEY You said your name was Harpenden.

HORTON *crosses to the door left.*

HARPENDEN That's right.

MULVANEY You mean you're Lord Harpenden?

HORTON *(turning at the door)* The Earl of Harpenden.

He exits.

MULVANEY So you're an earl?

HARPENDEN Er – yes – I'm afraid so.

MULVANEY Gosh! *(He moves to the armchair left centre and sits, still looking at* HARPENDEN.*)* Gosh, you're the first earl I ever saw.

HARPENDEN Oh, they're quite common, really, you know—

MULVANEY It's funny. You seemed quite an ordinary sort of guy.

HARPENDEN I am quite an ordinary sort of guy.

MULVANEY Don't give me that. You're an earl. Say, what do I call you?

HARPENDEN My friends usually call me Bobby.

MULVANEY I couldn't call you that.

HARPENDEN Why not?

MULVANEY It doesn't seem right.

HARPENDEN Last night you called me Dulcie.

MULVANEY *(ashamed)* Gosh! So I did.

HARPENDEN What's your Christian name?

MULVANEY Joe.

HARPENDEN Right. It's Joe and Bobby from now on. *(rising and crossing to him)* Now, listen, I've got to go and dress. *(He offers him a cigarette from the box on the phone table.)* How long is your leave?

MULVANEY Seven days.

HARPENDEN Where are you staying in London?

MULVANEY Nowhere yet. I only got up yesterday.

HARPENDEN Well, you can stay here if you like.

MULVANEY Hell, no... I couldn't.

HARPENDEN That's all right. I won't be here after to-morrow. I'm getting married, you see, and we're spending our leave together in Oxford.

MULVANEY *(rising, going level with him and shaking hands)* Gee, congratulations!

HARPENDEN Thanks, Joe.

MULVANEY *(lighting his cigarette)* What's that going to make her? I mean, what's the feminine of earl?

HARPENDEN Countess.

MULVANEY *(disappointed)* Oh, countess. I knew a girl became a countess. She married an Italian.

HARPENDEN Really?

MULVANEY She got herself a divorce, and now she's back in Elizabeth City, but she's still a countess.

HARPENDEN Well, of course, Italian countesses don't mean very much – I don't mean to be rude to your friend.

MULVANEY That's ok... Elly's a good girl, but she's not one of Nature's Countesses.

MULVANEY So much for Elly. Well, now it's settled, isn't it? You're going to stay here for your leave?

MULVANEY Well, it's darned kind of you... Bobby.

HARPENDEN My man, Horton, will look after you.

MULVANEY (giggling) Your man, Horton. Gee, this slays me! (He crosses to the settee, and sits centre.)

HARPENDEN smiles politely and moves up centre.

HARPENDEN Well, I must go and dress.

MULVANEY (rising) Just a minute. (He moves up to the doors centre.) Before I finally accept your very kind invitation, would it be all right to...well, you know, a guy might feel kind of lonely at times and...

HARPENDEN Yes, that's all right. Horton's very discreet.

MULVANEY It's a kind of hypothetical question, anyway. I don't know a darned soul in this town.

HARPENDEN Don't you? Oh well, we'll soon fix that. What's your type? Anything special? (He crosses down to the chair left centre, and picks up the phone.)

MULVANEY Under fifty!

HARPENDEN, now sitting on the chair, has begun to dial a number.

HARPENDEN I'm ringing up someone who's very good-looking, very amusing and mad about Americans.

MULVANEY crosses to him, then crosses to the settee.

(into the receiver) Hullo. Extension five-six-five-one, please. Thanks. (to MULVANEY) She works at the Air Ministry. Typist.

MULVANEY Yeah...a what?

HARPENDEN A typist.

MULVANEY Oh, stenographer, same thing. *(He sits.)*

HARPENDEN *(into the phone)* Hullo. Could I speak to Miss Crum, please? ...Lord Harpenden... *(to* MULVANEY*)* I'll ask her round for drinks and then you could ask her to supper or something... *(into the phone)* Hullo, Mabel... Bobby. How are you? *(He laughs.)* Well, I've told you before, never go out with Poles... Yes, I'm sure they're pets, but that's not the point... Look, darling, what time is that horrible old Sir Archibald letting you off today? ...Well, what on earth are you doing at the office if it's your day off? Oh, I see... What about coming round here for a drink? ...Albany... In about an hour... There's an American I want you to meet... Yes, he's a pet...he's a bombardier...he's got the most wonderful story about a raid on Bremen that'll thrill you to the marrow.

MULVANEY *shakes his head and says: "No".*

...All right, darling... I may be out, but he'll be here anyway... Yes, I'll try to be in, but I've got an interview at the Admiralty – I don't suppose it'll take long... That's the girl... Yes, tomorrow... St. George's, Hanover Square. You're coming, aren't you? ...Yes, you did. You met her at a cocktail party, about a year ago... Yes, that's right. Brown hair and grey eyes... Darling, you are speaking of the woman I love... Yes, I do, really I do... Yes, of course I love you too, but in a different way... *(He replaces the receiver quickly and crosses to* MULVANEY.*)* She's coming round this morning. She's got the day off, so you can ask her to lunch. *(He goes up to the door centre.)*

MULVANEY I've never done a raid on Bremen.

HARPENDEN *(vaguely)* Haven't you? Oh well, I don't suppose she'll mind.

MULVANEY Say, this is darned kind of you.

HARPENDEN Oh, that's all right. Just look on it as a bit of reciprocal lease-lend.

He exits to the bedroom.

MULVANEY *(rising and going to the doors centre. Calling)* Say, Bobby, can I use your phone?

HARPENDEN *(offstage)* Yes, of course.

MULVANEY *closes the door, goes above the phone table, and dials the number.*

MULVANEY   Hullo. Can I speak to Colonel Murphy, please? ...Lieutenant Mulvaney.

HORTON *enters left, and crosses to the bedroom doors up centre.*

HORTON   *(at the door)* Was your breakfast to your liking, sir?

MULVANEY   *(with an air of dignity, moving round the table to sit on the chair left centre)* Yes, thank you, Horton.

HORTON *raises his eyebrows and goes into the bedroom.*

(into the phone) Hullo, Spike? ...Say, listen, what happened to you guys last night? Yeah, I remember as far as that, but how come I got to a joint called the Jubilee all by myself? ...Oh, what was she like? ...Ok, I'll tell you, but you won't believe me. I slept in the same bed with an earl... No, not a girl, stupid, an earl! E-a-r-l, earl... Hell, no, I wouldn't fool you, Spike... *(angrily)* Because he says he's an earl... Well, you got to believe a guy when he says a thing like that... No, they don't wear crowns. Only when they go to Westminster Abbey.

HORTON *comes out of the bedroom with* MULVANEY's *uniform over his arm.*

I know that— *(He catches sight of* HORTON.*)* Hey, where are you going with my uniform?

HORTON   I was going to brush it, sir. If I may say so, it needs a good brushing badly.

MULVANEY   Righty-oh, old fellow. *(He giggles again.)*

HORTON *exits left.*

(into the phone) That was his man, Horton. Doesn't it slay you? ...The earl... Well, he's young...younger than me... You can too be an earl when you're young. Remember Little Lord Fauntleroy? ...Well, the little Duke, then... You're a disbelieving son of a bitch... A place called the Albany... sort of old-fashioned apartments, only the apartments are called chambers... Wise guy... Listen, Lord Byron lived here... Lord Byron... No, he's dead, you ignorant bastard. Don't you know anything except how to drive a B. Seventeen?

HORTON *re-enters left, and moves the stool left centre to its place down left. He lifts the tray before he speaks.*

This guy's called Harpenden – the Earl of Harpenden. Not a bad guy either. *(He catches sight of* HORTON.*)* A cracking good sort. See you down at the club. Ok. Goodbye. *(He rings off.)*

HORTON Excuse me, sir, do you want your buttons cleaned?

MULVANEY Er – no, thanks. We don't clean our buttons.

HORTON Very good, sir. *(He turns to go)*

MULVANEY Don't go for a minute. Stay and talk.

HORTON *(turning back)* Sir?

MULVANEY How long have you been the earl's man?

HORTON I've been with his Lordship all his life. Before that I was with his father.

MULVANEY You're not the only man he's got, I suppose?

HORTON No, sir. We have two large country estates, and before the war they needed a very big staff to keep them up.

MULVANEY Before the war? What's happened to them now?

HORTON One is a hospital, and the other has been taken over by the Air Force.

MULVANEY That's tough.

HORTON Tough, sir?

MULVANEY Well, I've read a lot about how these English aristocrats are being ruined by the war...

HORTON Oh no, sir. We are far from being ruined. Luckily our money does not come from our estates which were always run at a loss, even before the war.

MULVANEY What does it come from, then?

HORTON Ground rents, sir – in London, mostly.

MULVANEY Real estate, huh? That's pretty valuable, I guess—

HORTON Yes, sir, we must be worth all of two million pounds.

MULVANEY Holy smoke! Eight million dollars.

HORTON Yes, sir. Probably a good deal more than that.

> MULVANEY *whistles, rises and moves centre.* HORTON *waits patiently for his next question.*

MULVANEY You know, it doesn't seem right to me that a guy should be worth all that money and not have had to work for it.

HORTON It happens in your country too, sir.

MULVANEY Yeah, I suppose it does. Still, we don't call them earls.

HORTON No, sir.

MULVANEY You mustn't mind me. I'm just an ignorant American.

HORTON I'm an American myself, sir. I was born in America and had an American father.

MULVANEY Is that so?

HORTON My mother went to New York before I was born. She was a housemaid with the Morgan family there. She married an American opera singer.

MULVANEY She did? How come you're not at the Metropolitan yourself?

HORTON I fancy I inherited my mother's talents rather than my father's. Anyway, I understand he was not a very good opera singer. Well, now, sir, if you'll excuse me I'd better be getting on with my work. *(He moves up to the door left.)*

MULVANEY Sure thing. Sorry to have kept you.

HORTON Not at all, sir. Very glad of a chat with a fellow citizen.

He exits left. Left alone, MULVANEY looks round the room with a new expression on his face. He moves up to the desk up right and puts his cigarette out on the ashtray, his back to the stage centre.

MULVANEY *(muttering to himself)* Eight million bucks!

HARPENDEN comes out of the bedroom. He is dressed as an ordinary seaman, less boots. He has a cigarette in his mouth and goes to the telephone table for a match. He lights the cigarette. MULVANEY doesn't hear him as he makes no noise in his stocking soles. HARPENDEN crosses to MULVANEY at the desk.

HARPENDEN Do I need a shave?

MULVANEY turns, and starts when he sees the uniform.

MULVANEY Gosh Almighty!

HARPENDEN What's the matter?

MULVANEY Is that fancy dress, or are you really a gob?

HARPENDEN I'm really a gob. Tell me, do I need a shave?

MULVANEY *(examining his chin)* I guess it'll pass all right.

HARPENDEN *(doubtfully)* It's got to pass a lot of lynx-eyed old Admirals. *(He strokes his chin.)* Damn! I think I do need a shave.

MULVANEY Why don't you have a shave, then?

HARPENDEN *(crossing to the mirror down left)* I've only got one saw-toothed old razor blade, and I can't get another.

MULVANEY Not even for eight million dollars.

HARPENDEN (*opening the hall door, left. Calling*) Horton! Bring my boots down, will you?

MULVANEY Can you beat that – an earl being a gob.

HARPENDEN Do you mind not using that revolting word! We say "matelot".

MULVANEY Ok, matelot. Say, what sort of a ship are you in?

HARPENDEN Destroyer. (*He moves to the table behind the settee and picks up his wallet.*)

MULVANEY Seen any action?

HARPENDEN Not much. We sink the old submarine from time to time. We did have a bit of nonsense at Narvik once – a long time ago.

MULVANEY Say, that was a long time ago. How long have you been in this racket?

HARPENDEN Three years. (*He crosses to the telephone table, picks up a piece of paper and puts it in the wallet.*)

MULVANEY Gosh! And they haven't made you an officer yet?

HARPENDEN Not yet. They may this morning, though, that's what my interview at the Admiralty is about.

MULVANEY (*crossing down right*) How come you haven't been up for an interview before?

HARPENDEN I have been – three times. This is an annual ceremony.

MULVANEY And they turned you down – each time?

HARPENDEN (*sitting in the armchair left centre*) Flat, my dear lieutenant, as a pancake.

MULVANEY How come – you being his earlship and all that?

HARPENDEN His earlship and all that I may be, but as I am reluctantly forced to conclude, I am also an extremely incompetent sailor.

HORTON *enters left with boots, crosses above the chair to centre, and helps* HARPENDEN *to put them on.*

HORTON Your boots, my Lord.

HARPENDEN Thank you, Horton.

MULVANEY *watches this scene incredulously.*

MULVANEY For Pete's sake!

HARPENDEN You'd better get dressed, unless you want to receive Mabel Crum in your négligé.

MULVANEY Ok. *(He crosses towards the bedroom door, passing* HARPENDEN'S *chair as he does so. He halts abruptly at centre mock sternly.)* Isn't it customary in the British Navy for a rating to stand up when an officer passes him?

HARPENDEN, *grinning, rises smartly and stands to attention*

HARPENDEN I'm very sorry, sir.

MULVANEY So I should hope. *(He inspects him.)* All right. Carry on, me Lord. *(chuckling as he goes to the bedroom door)* Gee, wouldn't it slay you...

He exits. HARPENDEN *sits down again, while* HORTON *helps him on with the other boot.*

HORTON High-spirited young gentlemen, these Americans.

HARPENDEN Yes, Horton, very. By the way, you've got to look after him, after tomorrow. I'm lending him these chambers.

HORTON *(after a slight pause)* Is that quite wise, my Lord? You have some very breakable things here, and...

HARPENDEN Don't worry about that, Horton. He appreciates my things better than I do.

There is a ring at the front door.

HORTON *(rising)* Very good, my Lord.

He goes into the hall and after a second is heard greeting someone at the front door.

ELIZABETH *(offstage)* Good morning, Horton.

HORTON *(offstage)* Good morning, my Lady. *(re-entering)* Lady Elizabeth.

HARPENDEN *gets up as he hears their voices off stage and is standing up centre waiting for her.* **ELIZABETH** *enters.* **HORTON** *exits.*

ELIZABETH *is very young, and seemingly quite unconscious of the fact that she is very beautiful. She is in WAAF corporal's uniform.*

HARPENDEN Hullo, darling. *(He kisses her on the cheek.)* I told you – I've got to dash off for this interview in a second.

ELIZABETH I'm sorry, Bobby, but I just simply had to fly in and wish you luck.

HARPENDEN That's very sweet of you. I need it. Well, how are you? Poor little thing. Did you have an awful journey?

They cross together to the settee and sit, she at the right end, he at the left.

ELIZABETH Awful.

HARPENDEN Didn't you sleep at all?

ELIZABETH Not a wink.

HARPENDEN You look very well on it, I must say. *(He points to her arm.)* Hullo, haven't you gone down one? You were a sergeant last time I saw you.

ELIZABETH Yes, I know.

HARPENDEN What's the trouble?

ELIZABETH *(starting to comb her hair)* My CO's a cat.

HARPENDEN So's my captain, if it comes to that. Funny, we're neither of us awfully good at our jobs, are we?

ELIZABETH Oh, I'm quite good at mine. I just have bad luck. That's all.

HARPENDEN What did you do this time?

ELIZABETH I lost the plans of the Station Defence.

HARPENDEN Good Lord!

ELIZABETH Well, we found them again all right. I'd only left them in the Ladies'.

HARPENDEN Oh, but that's nothing at all. What bad luck!

ELIZABETH You're a beast, but I love you.

HARPENDEN (tying his bootlace) Do you really?

ELIZABETH Oh, I don't know about really.

HARPENDEN You're not beginning to have doubts on our wedding eve?

ELIZABETH No, Bobby, it's just that it's easier for you to know about these things than it is for me.

HARPENDEN Why, may I ask?

ELIZABETH Well, I've practically never known any other man in my life, except you – living up in that awful old Northern vastness of ours. (She is doing her hair during the speech.) I've always loved you, though, especially since you've been a sailor, because you look so beautiful in that uniform with those lovely baggy trousers and that low neck.

HARPENDEN Your view seems to be shared by their Lordships at the Admiralty.

ELIZABETH Now you – you've known hundreds of girls – thousands, probably.

HARPENDEN No, darling. Just hundreds.

ELIZABETH So it's easier for you to judge.

HARPENDEN Judge what?

ELIZABETH Whether you love me really or not.

HARPENDEN I love you really. *(He kisses her.)*

ELIZABETH More really than you love Mabel Crum?

HARPENDEN *(pause)* Who's Mabel Crum?

ELIZABETH You know very well who Mabel Crum is. So do I, too. We hear things, you know, even up in Inverness.

HARPENDEN *(rising and moving left)* I have simply no idea what you're talking about.

ELIZABETH Oh yes, you have. *(reproachfully)* Oh darling, how could you?

HARPENDEN How could I what?

ELIZABETH Mabel Crum. But she's awful.

HARPENDEN How do you know?

ELIZABETH Why, even Daddy knows her.

HARPENDEN I don't see why the fact that she's an acquaintance of Colonel the Duke of Ayr and Stirling should necessarily damn this lady, whoever she is.

ELIZABETH Well, you know what Daddy's like.

HARPENDEN Darling, you shock me...really you do.

ELIZABETH *takes a cigarette from the box on the table behind the settee.* HARPENDEN *goes behind the settee and gets a match from the table, and lights her cigarette.*

ELIZABETH Do you remember I met this Mabel Crum at a party when you were home on leave, about a year ago? I pretended not to know anything about it then, because we weren't even officially engaged. But I hear now you've been seeing her again.

HARPENDEN *(moving left centre)* Your gossip, my sweet, is as untrustworthy as your father's racing tips. I haven't seen Mabel Crum in months and months. *(He sits on the stool left of the settee)* In fact, I've really no idea what can possibly have happened to her. *(He glances furtively at his watch, then at the door.)*

ELIZABETH *(reproachfully)* Bobby! I always know when you're lying. You give yourself away every time.

HARPENDEN How?

ELIZABETH I'm not going to tell you how. It's a little trick that's going to come in very useful after we're married. After we're married I shall know the exact minute when you start seeing Mabel Crum again.

HARPENDEN Elizabeth! *(rising)* I consider that a perfectly revolting thing to say. Have you no moral standards of any sort?

ELIZABETH *(sincerely)* I don't know. I've never had a chance of finding out.

HARPENDEN And this is the girl I'm marrying!

ELIZABETH Oh. You don't have to worry about me. It's you I'm worrying about. I have a logical mind, and I can't see why, if you see Mabel Crum before we're married, you shouldn't see her after we're married, too.

HARPENDEN *(sitting on the settee beside her)* Shall I tell you why? A mere little bagatelle called the marriage vow.

ELIZABETH Do you mean to keep that little bagatelle?

HARPENDEN I do.

ELIZABETH *(staring at him)* Yes, I can see you do. You're not lying now. All right, darling, I'm sorry. *(She puts her head on his shoulder.)* It's only because I don't know anything about men. I've only got Daddy to go by.

HARPENDEN For the sake of the future of the human race, I trust that that is a misleading model.

ELIZABETH He's coming round here to see you this morning on business, he says.

HARPENDEN Oh God. Doesn't he ever do any work at the War Office?

ELIZABETH Not much. I think they only gave him the job because the Army wanted to take over Dunglennon.

HARPENDEN What is the job?

ELIZABETH Liaison Officer to the Poles.

HARPENDEN Oh, does he speak Polish?

ELIZABETH No, but he says he understands their point of view.

HARPENDEN I should have thought a little ready cash would have been more acceptable.

ELIZABETH Oh, he got that too. The bookies have got it by now. Which reminds me, darling, don't put any money into Zippy Snaps, will you?

HARPENDEN It's easy for you to sit there and say don't put any money into Zippy Snaps. Anyway, thank God, he'll miss me. I've got to go out. *(He sits up.)*

ELIZABETH Oh, Bobby, how awful, I've just remembered. I should have told you before. There's someone else coming round to see you this morning.

HARPENDEN *(leaning back again)* Yes, darling? Who's that?

ELIZABETH Well, I haven't only asked him to come round either.

HARPENDEN What do you mean?

ELIZABETH Well, I told you I had to sit up all night in the train, didn't I? Well, we were eight in the carriage, and next to me there was the most enchanting little Free French Lieutenant. Wasn't that funny?

HARPENDEN Hilarious.

ELIZABETH Well, anyway, we talked all night, in French mostly, so the others couldn't hear what we were saying.

HARPENDEN Darling, am I to understand that for ten hours you regaled each other with a selection of smutty stories?

ELIZABETH No, darling, but you know what Frenchmen are. We talked of all sorts of things – his private life, my private life, General Giraud... He said—

HARPENDEN Darling, will you kindly stop nattering and come to the point. *(He looks at his watch)*

ELIZABETH Oh yes, all right. Well, anyway, he was going up to London on leave, and the poor little man had no idea where he was going to stay, so I said...

HARPENDEN *grips her twist.*

What's the matter?

HARPENDEN So you said he could stop here?

ELIZABETH Yes, Bobby. I hope you don't mind, but I knew you wouldn't be using the flat after to-morrow, and I thought just for one night you wouldn't mind him bunking in that bed with you. *(She points to the bedroom door.)*

HARPENDEN Darling, there is already a vast American bombardier bunking in that bed with me. He's in there now, dressing. I refuse point-blank, for you or for Free France, to sleep three in a bed.

ELIZABETH Oh dear! Who's the American?

HARPENDEN It's far too long a story to tell you now. You say this is a little Frenchman?

ELIZABETH Quite little. Of course I only saw him sitting down.

HARPENDEN Would he fit on the sofa, do you think?

ELIZABETH Oh yes, I should think so.

HARPENDEN All right. *(rising.)* Well, you'd better stay here and explain the situation to him when he arrives. I've got to go. See you at lunch. Good-bye. *(He crosses to the door left. A thought strikes him. He looks nervously at the door, then turns back and crosses towards her.)* Or perhaps, now I come to think of it, it would be better if I just left a message for him with Horton. I mean, I don't want to keep you...

ELIZABETH That's all right. I'd like to stay here. I've got nothing to do all morning.

HARPENDEN Oh, splendid! *(a pause)* Darling, do you mind if I make a phone call?

ELIZABETH I thought you were in a hurry.

HARPENDEN *(dialling a number with his back to her, as he speaks)* Yes, but this is something I've just thought of that's got to be done. Official business – for my captain. *(into the phone)* Hullo, Air Ministry. Extension five-six-five-one, please... Hullo... Oh, this is Lord Harpenden. Could I possibly speak to the young lady I spoke to earlier this morning? ...I forget her name... Oh yes, how stupid of me... *(to* ELIZABETH*)* Terrible head for names. *(into the phone)* Oh, hullo ...Yes, this is Lord Harpenden. You may remember I spoke to you earlier on a certain matter. I see that you've taken no steps to expedite delivery... Yes, I'm glad of that... Well, the fact is that something has just cropped up that renders the immediate project temporarily inoperative... Yes, that's exactly it...exactly... I'll ring you again. Goodbye.

He bangs down the receiver.

ELIZABETH *(without suspicion)* What have you got to do with the Air Ministry, darling?

HARPENDEN Oh, we work a lot with the R.A.F., you know... Coastal Command, flying boats... Co-operation's the thing these days. *(He looks at his watch.)* Oh Lord, I'm late. Goodbye, darling. *(He kisses her.)*

The doorbell rings.

Oh, Lord, here's your Frenchman. You can entertain him.

DUKE *(offstage)* Good morning, Horton.

HORTON *(offstage)* Good morning, your Grace.

ELIZABETH No, it's not. It's Daddy.

HARPENDEN Damn!

HORTON *opens the door left.*

HORTON His Grace.

The **DUKE** *enters. He is in brigadier's uniform, about fifty-five, rather portly, but with remnants of great good looks.*

DUKE *(crossing to centre)* Ah, hullo, my boy. I've found you in. Good. How are you? Looking well, anyway. All that ozone, I expect, isn't that it?

HARPENDEN Yes, sir. Thank you. If you'll excuse me, I must...

DUKE That's all right, my boy. *(crossing down centre)* I won't keep you a second. Just wanted a little chat on certain rather pressing matters...business, you know – awful bore and all that, but it's no good shirking these things, what?

ELIZABETH *(crossing up to them)* Daddy, Bobby's got an interview at the Admiralty, if he doesn't start soon he'll be late.

DUKE What's that? Mustn't be late for the Admiralty, my boy. That'll never do!

HARPENDEN No, sir. I quite agree. *(He starts to go.)*

DUKE *(holding arm and drawing him back)* So I'll come straight to the point. *(He sits in the armchair left centre.)* I've just come from your solicitors. We've been looking over that marriage settlement. Well now, that's a very handsome document, I must say, a very handsome document indeed.

HARPENDEN Do you mind, sir, if we talk about it some other time? If I'm late for this interview any chance of promotion...

DUKE Quite so, my boy, but this won't take a minute. Who's the president of your interviewing board?

HARPENDEN I've really no idea.

DUKE Well, find out his name, and if you're late I'll give him a tinkle this afternoon and explain you were with me.

HARPENDEN Thank you, sir. That's very kind of you, but...

DUKE That's all right, my boy. No trouble at all. I know all these old admirals. They're ten a penny at Boodle's... Do anything for me – most of 'em. Now, where were we? Ah, yes – the settlement. Now here's where I think it falls down. I notice that no provision whatever has been made for your wife's family.

HARPENDEN That was agreed, sir.

DUKE Agreed by whom? Not by me.

HARPENDEN No, sir. You weren't consulted. By your daughter's solicitors.

DUKE Quite so – but I must say they seem to me to have slipped up badly there. Now there are one or two most deserving cases in our family that need attention...for instance, Elizabeth's Aunt Amy.

ELIZABETH Daddy... Aunt Amy's perfectly all right in that nursing home – and she's got plenty of money of her own...

DUKE Quite so, my dear, but she could always do with a bit more.

ELIZABETH I can't see why, seeing that she thinks she's Karl Marx.

DUKE That hallucination is unfortunate, I know, but should not, I feel, preclude her from ending her days in a manner fitting to her true estate. However, if you like, we can leave Aunt Amy out. Now – coming a little nearer home...

ELIZABETH *gives* HARPENDEN *a "look".*

HARPENDEN I made no provision for you, sir, because, as you know, I had anyway agreed to make you an allowance.

DUKE Quite so, my boy, quite so, but these things are better on paper. On paper, my boy, signed, sealed and delivered.

ELIZABETH *rises.*

HARPENDEN I can't see why...

DUKE My dear fella, these days we must face facts...

ELIZABETH *(pointing at her watch)* Bobby!

HARPENDEN Oh Lord, I'm going to be late, please can we face them some other time? *(moving to go)*

DUKE *(rising)* I'll tell you what, I've got a car and I'll drive you round to the Admiralty *(He moves round the chair and goes from centre to the door left.)* and we can talk some more about it on the way. What about that, eh?

HARPENDEN *(already out in the hall)* Thank you, sir, only we must start now!

DUKE Yes, yes, that's all right. *(He suddenly remembers and turns back to the telephone, sitting on the chair left centre again.)* By Jove, I nearly forgot.

ELIZABETH *(frantically)* Oh, Daddy, do please hurry...

DUKE That's all right, my dear. Don't worry...

HARPENDEN *re-appears with his hat – inscribed "HMS" – on his head.*

ELIZABETH But Bobby's got an interview at the Admiralty.

HARPENDEN Oh Lord! What's happened now? *(He takes a cigarette from the box on the phone table and lights it.)*

DUKE Just a little tinkle, my boy. I won't keep you a second. *(dialling)*

ELIZABETH Don't worry, darling.

DUKE *(into the phone)* Hullo, is that Macdougall and Steinbeck? ...This is Primrose Path speaking... Primrose Path... Yes, that's right... I want fifty pounds each way Bern... What's that? ...Oh well, it's in the post. Yes, posted it myself... My dear sir, I can assure you... Oh, the old account? ...Ah well, there was a little mistake over that. My servant forgot to post it... Yes, devilish stupid of him... My good man, *(sitting up)* I presume you know who you're talking to? ...Oh, you do? ...Well, really, that's nice treatment, I must say... Very well, then. I shall remove my custom elsewhere... *(He rings off furiously.)* Bolsheviks! *(He begins to dial another number.)*

HARPENDEN Oh God!

ELIZABETH Daddy...

DUKE Macdougall and Steinbeck, gad, I'll have those two ruffians called up. *(into the phone)* Hullo, Boodle's? Give me the hall porter, please... Hullo, Barker? This is the Duke of Ayr and Stirling... I want half a crown each way on Bernadotte in the three-thirty. What's that? ... *(impatiently)* Yes, yes, when I see you. *(He rings off.)* Tiresome fellow.

The doorbell rings. The **DUKE** *rises and crosses between* **ELIZABETH** *and* **HARPENDEN**.

All right, my boy. Now we can go. Are you quite ready?

HARPENDEN Yes, sir, quite. *(He moves towards the door left.)*

DUKE Hey, wait a minute! You can't go to the Admiralty looking like a scarecrow.

He pulls **HARPENDEN**'s *collar about.* **HARPENDEN** *gives a wail and runs to* **ELIZABETH**.

HARPENDEN Here, you fix it.

ELIZABETH *smoothes his collar.*

HORTON *(offstage)* What name, sir?

COLBERT *(offstage)* Lieutenant Colbert.

ELIZABETH There, darling. It looks sweet.

HORTON *enters left.*

HORTON Lieutenant Colbert.

HARPENDEN God in Heaven! *(He moves up centre.)*

COLBERT *enters. He is a small, clean shaven, very neat-looking officer in the Fighting French Forces.* **HARPENDEN** *shakes hands with him.*

Hullo. How are you? Lovely to see you. Make yourself at home. I've got to go.

He disappears into the hall, leaving COLBERT *standing, looking after him in a rather surprised fashion. Then he bows to* ELIZABETH.

ELIZABETH *(crossing to the door left between the* DUKE *and* COLBERT*)* Hullo. This is my father – Lieutenant Colbert. Daddy, hurry up. *(She runs off left.)*

DUKE *(with an atrocious accent)* Enchanté, Monsieur, enchanté.

He shakes hands with COLBERT, *who comes centre to meet him.*

Il fait chaud aujourd'hui, n'est-ce pas?

COLBERT Oui, Monsieur. Je l'ai remarqué moi-même.

DUKE Votre figure me semble familier. Vous connaissez Paris?

COLBERT Oui, Monsieur. Je connais Paris.

DUKE I haven't been to Paris since the Duke de Gaze won the Grand Prix. Ah, Paris in the spring! The boulevards, the restaurants, the cafés...

COLBERT Les jolies femmes?

DUKE Ah, les jolies femmes. I remember when I was there last, a charming little thing...une morceau charmant...

COLBERT *(not understanding)* Comment?

DUKE Une pièce...

HARPENDEN *and* ELIZABETH *dash in from left.*

HARPENDEN For heaven's sake, sir!

ELIZABETH Daddy!

DUKE All right, my boy, I'm coming.

HARPENDEN *and* ELIZABETH *exit.*

We must meet again, monsieur. Il faut que vous devenir manger avec moi, un soir, à mon club, Turf!

COLBERT Avec plaisir.

DUKE *(in French)* Capitale. *(He goes to the door left. To* **ELIZABETH** *as she is standing just inside the door)* I'll pick you up later, my dear.

He exits.

(offstage) Now, my boy...

ELIZABETH *shuts the door and moves to sit in the chair left centre.*

(offstage) Now the point about this settlement, my boy, is that it's a form of insurance...

ELIZABETH Sit down, won't you? *(She sits.)*

COLBERT *(sitting at the left end of the settee)* Thank you.

ELIZABETH It's all right about using this flat, except that you'll have to sleep on the sofa just for tonight.

COLBERT That is very kind. Who was that sailor?

ELIZABETH That was my fiancé – Bobby Harpenden.

COLBERT Your fiancé?

ELIZABETH You're surprised?

COLBERT You told me he was an earl. I had not expected to see him dressed in that manner.

ELIZABETH You pictured him with a little coronet and an ermine cloak?

COLBERT Hardly, milady. But I imagined him a little older, and with a big moustache and a hooked nose... I do not know why.

ELIZABETH He's very good-looking, don't you think?

COLBERT Not for me. No, no, no, no. He is altogether too... qu'est-ce que c'est fâde?

ELIZABETH Insipid.

COLBERT Yes, too insipid.

ELIZABETH Oh.

COLBERT I am sorry, milady, but I must say what I think.

ELIZABETH That's quite all right, only do you mind not calling me milady?

COLBERT I beg your pardon. What must I call you, then?

ELIZABETH Well, later on last night we were calling each other Elizabeth and René.

COLBERT Last night was...last night.

ELIZABETH And today's today. I don't see what difference...

COLBERT Milady – Elizabeth – I made one of two errors last night. Either I said to you too much...or I did not say enough.

ELIZABETH Well, you didn't say too much.

COLBERT Then I did not say enough.

ELIZABETH What more did you have to say?

COLBERT Very much more indeed.

ELIZABETH Then say it now.

COLBERT You would be very angry with me if I did. No, it is better I keep silent.

There is silence. **COLBERT** *suddenly slaps his knee and gets up.*

I shall say it. I must say it. *(He crosses to her.)* Elizabeth – do not marry this man.

ELIZABETH Not marry Bobby? Why ever not?

COLBERT I implore you. Turn back before it is too late.

ELIZABETH But...but I love him. Why should I...

COLBERT You love him. Yes. *(crossing down left)* You told me so last night. But you also told me what is the truth – you told me you had for him no – no passion, no white-hot burning of the heart.

ELIZABETH Oh dear! Did I really say that?

COLBERT *(crossing up to her)* You did not employ those words, but that is nevertheless what you said. You love him – oh yes, we will agree. So does one love one's brother or one's little puppy dog. But you are not in love with him. No, no, no, milady, Elizabeth. Not in a thousand years.

ELIZABETH But I may be in love with him. It's just that I don't know, that's all. Anyway, ordinary, quiet, restful love is a much better basis for marriage than this white-hot burning passion of the heart...

COLBERT Oh no, Elizabeth. Oh no. *(crossing up centre)* That is where you make such a terrible mistake. Ah, I see it all so clearly. Two great English houses, the alliance planned from an age when you were both little children, obedient little children...

ELIZABETH No, no, it's not like that at all. Both of us have always been perfectly free to choose.

COLBERT That is what your families have allowed you to believe.

ELIZABETH But – even if I'm not in love with Bobby – and I don't admit that for a minute, mind you – but even if I'm not, at least he's in love with me.

COLBERT Is he? *(crossing to her)* And what about the woman Crum?

ELIZABETH Oh dear! Did I tell you that?

COLBERT *(kneeling beside her)* Turn back, Elizabeth. Turn back, or you will ruin two lives.

ELIZABETH *(rising)* But this is ridiculous. What right have you to say these things to me?

COLBERT *(rising)* There! I told you you would be angry.

ELIZABETH *(walking slowly upstage and then down again during the speech)* I'm not in the least angry, but the whole thing is quite absurd. Supposing I don't marry Bobby – what then? I go back to Inverness, and after the war I'll go on living in Dunglennon, and I'll never meet anybody as nice or as good-looking or as – all right – as rich as Bobby – and I'll just be an old maid and sink into a decline. *(She, is now standing centre facing him.)*

COLBERT *(taking a step towards her)* You will not be an old maid. Nor will you sink into a decline. It is not in your face. *(He comes closer to her)* You are very beautiful, but that is nothing. You have in your eyes a joy, a desire, a voluptuous flame of life that will not be quenched.

ELIZABETH Have I?

COLBERT Wait, Elizabeth. Wait, and one day you will find a lover worthy of those eyes.

ELIZABETH How do you know I will?

COLBERT *(taking another step towards her)* I know it. That is all. You have only to wait. And I know too that you will not need to wait for very long.

There is a pause while ELIZABETH *evidently ponders what line she ought to pursue.*

ELIZABETH Look here, what reason have you got for saying all this to me?

COLBERT That is a question I do not wish to answer.

ELIZABETH I believe you're making love to me.

COLBERT You have the right to believe that, milady.

ELIZABETH I'm going to tell Bobby every single thing you've said.

COLBERT Very well. *(He moves down right, turns, and faces her.)* He will strike me with a right hook, and that is unfortunate but...

ELIZABETH I hope he does strike you with a right hook – and a left hook too...

COLBERT *(resignedly. Crossing back to her)* You see how angry I have made you. If what I said was not the truth, you would not be angry, you would merely laugh.

ELIZABETH I do laugh. I think everything you've said is frightfully funny. *(rather tearfully)* I may not be laughing outside, but I am laughing inside – like mad.

A pause.

COLBERT I will go. *(He moves up to the door left. Then, he turns and comes back.)* I repeat. Turn back, Elizabeth, before it is too late. Leave this earl, who does not love you, to his title, his riches and his Crams.

ELIZABETH Oh, go away.

COLBERT *goes out left.*

ELIZABETH *is plainly upset. She blows her nose violently, then crosses left, and turns the radiogram on.*

After a slight pause there comes the strain of a dance band playing a soft sentimental air.

MULVANEY *comes out of the bedroom, whistling cheerfully. He is dressed in American Army uniform with wings. He stops short at the sight of* ELIZABETH. *He looks her up and down appraisingly, and a slow smile of satisfaction spreads across his face.*

MULVANEY Well, well, well. So you finally showed up.

ELIZABETH *(nervously)* Hullo. *(She turns off the radio.)*

MULVANEY I guess I'd better introduce myself. My name's Mulvaney – Lieutenant Mulvaney.

ELIZABETH *(moving towards centre)* How do you do. I'm...

MULVANEY *(shaking hands)* That's ok. You don't have to tell me who you are. Your pal the earl told me all about you.

ELIZABETH *(politely)* He told me about you, too.

MULVANEY Yeah, I know. *(He walks round, taking her in, with undisguised admiration.)* Well, well, well. I'm telling you that son of a gun didn't exaggerate one little bit. In fact he didn't tell me the half of it. *(after another appraising stare)* Zowie!

ELIZABETH *(smiling nervously)* Thank you very much.

MULVANEY Amongst other things he said you had a soft spot for Americans.

ELIZABETH Did he? *(crossing to centre)* Well, of course, I like Americans very much.

MULVANEY *(following her round)* Then I can see you and me are going to be friends.

ELIZABETH I hope so.

MULVANEY Strictly between ourselves – I got a soft spot too – for babes who look like you.

ELIZABETH That's splendid. *(She moves away.)*

MULVANEY It's terrific. Say, how about a little drink? I could do with one myself.

ELIZABETH *(faintly)* So could I. *(She sits on the settee.)*

MULVANEY Fine! *(going up towards the table up left)* I wonder where the earl keeps his liquor – if any.

ELIZABETH *(pointing up right)* In that cupboard over there.

MULVANEY Yeah. *(He goes to the desk cupboard, and opens it.)* You'd know a thing like that, wouldn't you? Who better? *(He takes out a bottle of Scotch.)* Hot dog! Here's some Scotch.

He crosses to the table up left and pours out two drinks.

ELIZABETH Isn't there any sherry?

MULVANEY Sherry? You wouldn't fool me, would you, babe? You'll take Scotch and like it. *(He lifts up the glasses.)*

ELIZABETH *(seeing how much is in the glass)* Oh, I couldn't possibly drink that. Would you mind...

MULVANEY Spoiling it for you? Ok. *(He squirts a minute portion of soda water into the glass and carries it to her at the settee. He brings his own glass with him.)*

ELIZABETH But it's still much too strong.

MULVANEY Aw, go on. It won't hurt you. *(He raises his glass.)* Here's to Anglo-American relations.

ELIZABETH *(after a pause, muttering)* Anglo-American relations.

They drink. MULVANEY *drinks his in one gulp.* ELIZABETH *takes a sip of hers and makes a face.*

MULVANEY What's the matter?

ELIZABETH It's so strong.

MULVANEY *(sitting beside her on the settee)* Aw now, you wouldn't want me to think you a cissy, would you – in that uniform ? Go on, drink it – for the honour of the RAF.

ELIZABETH, *obeying a sudden impulse, swallows the whole drink. She splutters.* MULVANEY *takes the glass from her and with his own puts them on the stool left of the settee.*

That's better.

ELIZABETH *(weakly)* I'm not used to drinks as strong as that at this time in the morning.

MULVANEY *(smiling)* Yeah, yeah. I know, I know. *(having put the glasses down)* Well, well. Now what shall we do?

ELIZABETH I don't know.

MULVANEY You haven't any etchings to show me?

ELIZABETH Bobby has some in his bedroom.

MULVANEY Yeah. I bet he has.

He laughs as if he has made a joke. ELIZABETH *laughs too, politely, but puzzled.*

He didn't tell me you'd be in uniform. It suits you, though. Gosh, that blue brings out the colour of your eyes.

ELIZABETH Oh! Do you think so?

MULVANEY I certainly do. That's one fine little pair of eyes you got yourself there, Sergeant. *(looking at her arm)* Are you a sergeant?

ELIZABETH No. Just a corporal.

MULVANEY Not for long, I'll bet. Say, aren't all the air marshals crazy about you?

ELIZABETH They don't appear to be.

MULVANEY They must be a lot of blind old sourpusses. Now, if you were in the Army Air Corps...

ELIZABETH What would happen?

MULVANEY You'd be a general.

ELIZABETH I wish I were in the Army Air Corps.

MULVANEY *(moving nearer her)* You're not the only one who wishes that. Tell me, babe, what do you like most about Americans?

ELIZABETH Well, I've met so awfully few, working where I do. But if you're typical of them, then I've got to admit that... *(She stops.)*

MULVANEY Go ahead. Admit what?

ELIZABETH Well – that they're a bit – different from other men.

MULVANEY Different in a good way or a bad way?

ELIZABETH *(after a slight pause)* In a good way.

MULVANEY *(jumping up and going to the drinks table)* Ok. So let's have another drink.

ELIZABETH *(rising)* Oh, no...please.

MULVANEY (*pouring out drinks*) Say, listen – you're not fooling anyone, babe, but yourself with this Pollyanna stuff. I want another drink, you want another drink, so we both have another little drink. It's good stuff too – pre-war, by the smell of it. (*He goes back to her and hands her a drink.*) Bottoms up this time – or as you say – no heel-taps.

ELIZABETH Oh dear. I'd much rather not.

MULVANEY Say, listen, if you haven't finished that drink by the time I've finished mine, I'll put you over my knee and spank the life out of you.

ELIZABETH I believe you would, too.

MULVANEY You bet your sweet life I would. Now— (*He extends his glass.*) here's to even closer Anglo-American relations.

ELIZABETH (*turning away from him, muttering*) Even closer Anglo-American relations. (*She closes her eyes and gulps it down quickly. Proudly*) There! (*She suppresses a belch.*) Who's a cissy now? (*She sits, hurriedly.*)

MULVANEY (*admiringly*) Not you, babe. (*He takes her glass and puts it with his own on the stool.*) Ok. Shall I tell you about Bremen?

ELIZABETH (*turning her head slowly, and smiling*) Oh yes, do.

MULVANEY Well, (*a demonstrating gesture*) there we were, upside down, nothing on the clock, enemy fighters swarming all around us...

ELIZABETH Oh, how awful!

MULVANEY So what did we do?

ELIZABETH What?

MULVANEY Come a little closer and I'll tell you.

ELIZABETH (*moving nearer to him – a trifle thickly*) What did you do?

MULVANEY We righted the ship, beat off the fighters, and returned to our base.

ELIZABETH Riddled with holes.

MULVANEY Riddled with holes.

ELIZABETH How wonderful.

MULVANEY Aw, it didn't mean a thing.

ELIZABETH Oh, but it did. It was wonderful. Did you get the... the congrenshenal thing?

MULVANEY Come again?

ELIZABETH *(carefully)* The Congressional Medal of Honour.

MULVANEY Oh, that? No, as a matter of fact they're thinking up something else for us.

ELIZABETH Isn't that wonderful?

MULVANEY Oh, it was nothing. *(He puts his hand on her knee.)*

She beams at him, and then appears to be conscious for the first time of his hand on her knee. She stares at it more puzzled than angry. MULVANEY *jumps up and goes to the radiogram.*

How do you work this thing? You should know.

ELIZABETH Oh yes, I do. I'll show you. *(She rises and crosses rather unsteadily to the radiogram.)*

She turns on the radiogram, the music comes fading in. MULVANEY *holds out his arms to her in invitation to dance, and she goes to him. They begin to dance, moving towards down centre.*

MULVANEY Gosh, baby, you're one of the loveliest things I ever saw in all my life, and I'm not kidding.

ELIZABETH You're rather lovely yourself.

He kisses her. The telephone bell rings. She struggles for a second, then succumbs and finally contributes. It is a long kiss. The telephone bell rings two or three times, unnoticed. Then MULVANEY *breaks away.*

MULVANEY *(going to the phone)* I suppose I'd better answer that.

ELIZABETH *stands in apparent ecstasy, then starts to dance slowly across to right.*

(into the phone) Hullo. No, he's out. Who? ...Mabel who? *(A look of horror crosses his face.)* Yeah, I'll tell him... What was that name again? Yeah, that's what it sounded like. *(He bangs the receiver down quickly, and stands to attention above the phone table. He stares at ELIZABETH with horror and perplexity)*

ELIZABETH *(moving towards him in her dance. Drowsily)* Who was that?

MULVANEY No one. No one at all.

ELIZABETH *(close to him)* Don't you want to go on dancing?

MULVANEY *(burbling)* No, I've got to rush, you know...this minute...see my colonel... *(By this time he is out of the door which he shuts behind him.)*

ELIZABETH *looks a little surprised, then, smiling, moves back to the settee and sits on the corner right, rather suddenly, her legs straight out in front of her.*

The DUKE *comes in, smiling contentedly. He is wearing his hat and carrying his stick and gloves.*

DUKE Ah, there you are, my dear. I'm sorry I kept you waiting. I hope you haven't been bored?

ELIZABETH *(drowsily)* No, Daddy. I wasn't bored. Not bored at all. Not even the teeniest little bit bored. *(She pulls the cushion down and lies down on the settee.)* Good night, Daddy, I'm going to sleep.

The DUKE *moves a step back and, puzzled, looks down at his daughter, already sleeping.*

DUKE God bless my soul! What an astonishing thing!

Curtain.

ACT II

Scene. The same.

Time. About 11 p.m. the same night.

The curtain rises to disclose a man and a woman sitting together in the armchair left centre. The man can be recognized as **JOE MULVANEY**. *The woman,* **MABEL CRUM**. *She has a glass of gin in her hand, and he a glass of whisky. They both look extremely bored.*

HARPENDEN *enters from the hall, throwing his latchkeys on the table up left.*

HARPENDEN *(carelessly, as he passes the chair)* Hullo, Mabel.

MULVANEY *jumps up hastily, almost spilling* **MABEL CRUM** *on to the floor. She is a little older than* **ELIZABETH**, *but with an even wider, an even more innocent, stare of her eyes.*

MABEL *(moving right)* Hullo, darling.

HARPENDEN *moves left to the table up left and gets himself a drink.* **MULVANEY** *moves down left.*

MULVANEY *(embarrassed)* I didn't think you'd be back till later.

HARPENDEN I'm sorry, Joe. I went on a pub crawl all by myself and got bored. All my friends are out of town.

MABEL What about Freddie Dawson?

HARPENDEN His leave's been cancelled. He went dashing back this afternoon.

MABEL Wasn't he going to be your best man?

HARPENDEN Yes, he was. I knew it was a mistake to choose a commando. *(moving down centre)* Joe, what about you deputizing for him?

MULVANEY *(moving towards* HARPENDEN; *uncomfortably)* Well – it's darned kind of you, Bobby – and I sure appreciate the compliment – but maybe I'd better not.

HARPENDEN Why not?

MULVANEY Well – I'm an American and perhaps your family wouldn't like it.

HARPENDEN I've told you I haven't got any family, except a very old grandmother who can't move out of her bed, and sends me an egg from time to time.

MULVANEY It's your wife's family I meant.

HARPENDEN They won't mind. In fact they'd be delighted.

MULVANEY *(nervously)* No, Bobby. I don't think they'd be delighted.

HARPENDEN Why not? It's an excellent gesture towards closer Anglo-American relations.

MULVANEY Yeah. You're telling me. Hell, Bobby, I'd just love to do it ordinarily, and I'm grateful for you asking me, but count me out, there's a good guy.

HARPENDEN Oh, all right. What about you, Mabel? *(crossing right to behind the settee)* I could dress you up as a sailor.

MABEL Darling, I couldn't trust myself. I might break down and cry and tear the bride's eyes out.

HARPENDEN Isn't she a nice girl, Joe? Don't you adore her? *(He moves to the left end of the settee.)*

MULVANEY *(without enthusiasm)* Yeah, I sure do.

MABEL He doesn't. He thinks I'm torture.

HARPENDEN *(moving behind the settee)* That wasn't what he appeared to be thinking when I came in.

MABEL *(at the right end of the settee)* Darling, he'd been getting something out of my eye!

HARPENDEN For a girl who takes care of her appearance, Mabel, you manage to get an inordinate amount of things in your eye.

MULVANEY *(to* MABEL*)* Now listen, what do you mean I think you're torture? I don't know what...

MABEL He's fallen in love with a girl he met this morning.

MULVANEY *(alarmed)* Hey! *(crossing centre)* That's not true. Whatever gave you that idea?

HARPENDEN *sits on the stool left of the settee.*

MABEL He won't stop talking about how lovely she was, and how melting and soft and alluring; and then apparently he made an awful boob, because he blushes scarlet whenever he thinks of it.

MULVANEY Hey, listen...

HARPENDEN Who was she?

MULVANEY Oh, no one. No one at all. I was making it all up.

MABEL It was a WAAF.

HARPENDEN Tell us about it, Joe.

MULVANEY Listen, Bobby. Have a heart, will you? Don't ask me about it. It's something I'm trying to forget.

MABEL Not very hard.

HARPENDEN He probably fell for the old confidence trick... You know, the furious father or the enraged fiancé or something.

MULVANEY Stop it, will you? Tell us about yourself. How did the interview go? I forgot to ask you on the phone this morning...

HARPENDEN *shakes his head gloomily.*

What went wrong?

HARPENDEN In the first place I was a quarter of an hour late, then I found myself overdoing the free, frank, open, boyish manner and got the jitters and became far too servile and cringing, and my hair was too long and I hadn't shaved and I didn't know how many twopenny-halfpenny stamps I could buy for half a crown. In short, for the fourth time in this war, I proved conclusively both to the Admiralty and to myself that I am not the officer type.

MULVANEY Too bad. *(cautiously, moving down left)* Tell me, did you see your fiancée today?

HARPENDEN Only for a few seconds – at Brown's about drink time. I was supposed to meet her for lunch, but she rang up to say she had a headache and had gone to bed.

MULVANEY *(straightening his tie)* Headache, huh? *(heartily)* Well, well. Do you know what I think I'm going to do? *(going up to the doors centre)* I'm going to bye-byes myself.

HARPENDEN And leave me alone with this man-eater on my wedding eve?

MULVANEY Aw, she's no man-eater. You don't get real man-eaters this side of the Atlantic.

HARPENDEN *(to* MABEL*)* If I were you, darling, I'd resent that.

MABEL Americans always fall for the obvious. They don't appreciate subtlety.

MULVANEY If you want to see a real man-eater you come to Elizabeth City and I'll show you one.

HARPENDEN Who? Dulcie?

MULVANEY Hell, no. Not Dulcie. I meant – Elly.

HARPENDEN Oh, Countess Elly.

MULVANEY Dulcie's a good girl. I'm in love with Dulcie— *(as an afterthought)* I hope. *(He opens the bedroom door. Contritely, to* MABEL*)* Gee – Miss Crum – I must be going nuts. I forgot all about seeing you home.

MABEL That's all right, Lieutenant. I can easily see myself home.

MULVANEY But – hell – you live outside London – in a village called Kensington or something, don't you?

HARPENDEN All right, Joe, don't worry, I'll see she gets home all right. You go on off to bed.

MULVANEY Ok. Good night, folks. *(He goes into the bedroom.)*

HARPENDEN *(rising and moving up to the doors centre)* Use the side nearest the window. And don't take up all the bed, like you did last night. I spent half the night squashed against the wall, struggling for breath.

MULVANEY *(his head appearing through the door)* Last night I thought you were Dulcie.

HARPENDEN Well, tonight you'll oblige me by thinking I'm Hitler.

MULVANEY Ok. Just so long as I know. *(His head disappears.)*

HARPENDEN *(moving to behind the settee)* What do you think of him?

MABEL He's a pet.

HARPENDEN That is a term you apply without any discrimination to any member of the Allied Forces who happens to look your way. I asked you what you thought of him?

MABEL Why so interested?

HARPENDEN Because, if you must know, I think it's time you settled down and took to yourself a nice husband.

MABEL Darling – not an American.

HARPENDEN Why not?

MABEL You don't *marry* Americans.

HARPENDEN Don't you? Oh well – you know best.

MABEL Anyway – what about Dulcie?

HARPENDEN Dulcie's three thousand miles away.

MABEL *(sincerely)* Poor Dulcie!

HARPENDEN Poor Dulcie. Did you have a good time tonight? What did you do?

MABEL Oh, we went to the Hippodrome and had dinner at the Savoy. He was really awfully sweet. Very distrait though. I think he really did have some rather shattering experience this morning.

HARPENDEN Really?

MABEL The poor pet was in such a state about it – whatever it was – that he wanted to dash off after dinner to the park, or somewhere and think things out, he said.

HARPENDEN Isn't that typically American – to go to the park and think things out?

MABEL He didn't want to come back here at all – until I said you'd be awfully offended with him if he just faded away without saying a word. And even then he was terribly nervous and jumpy. I couldn't get him to settle down at all.

HARPENDEN Sorry to have come barging in on you like that.

MABEL Oh, that's quite all right, darling. Between you and me I think we were both of us delighted to see you barge in.

HARPENDEN I'm sorry about that. Why?

MABEL Well – he – because he doesn't like me so much and I – because I love you so much.

HARPENDEN I bet you say that to all the sailors. (He goes up to the drinks table to refill his glass.)

MABEL Not every sailor is as sweet as you are. And not every sailor has two million pounds tucked away in his ditty-box.

HARPENDEN Only until nasty Mr. Gallacher takes it out of my ditty-box.

MABEL Yes, but what fun you can have with it until he does. What fun you have had!

HARPENDEN turns, and drinks.

HARPENDEN That'll be my epitaph when I swing from the lamp post outside Albany.

MABEL You have got a morbid sense of humour, darling.

HARPENDEN *(crossing down centre)* Look, it wasn't only because I was bored I came back early tonight. I wanted to see you.

MABEL Did you – darling?

HARPENDEN *(embarrassed)* Yes. Well. First I was going to write you – then I thought that was a bit – you know – then I thought I ought to tell you – myself – although it isn't awfully easy – so—

MABEL *looks at him sympathetically.* HARPENDEN *turns away, in order not to meet her eyes.*

You see, we've always been good friends and I'd hate anything – Oh God! I wish I could come to the point.

MABEL *(quietly)* You don't have to, darling. I know what the point is. After tonight, you don't want to see me any more. That's it, isn't it?

HARPENDEN *(after a pause, crossing to her)* You're an angel.

MABEL But – darling – don't be silly. I knew perfectly well. I don't see you very often – you get so little leave anyway, and when I read you were getting married I thought, well, that's that. He'll just fade quietly away and I won't ever see him again. I didn't even expect a letter – because anyway you're not a very good letter writer, are you? I'm awfully grateful you should have told me, though.

HARPENDEN I didn't tell you. You told me.

MABEL You tried to, anyway. *(rising)* Can I get myself another drink? *(She moves to the drinks table up left.)*

HARPENDEN Yes, of course.

HARPENDEN *moves to the desk, takes out a ready written cheque, picks up* MABEL'*s bag from the table behind the settee and is putting the cheque in the bag when she turns in time to see him.*

MABEL What on earth are you up to? *(She crosses to him, takes the bag, returns to centre, takes the cheque out and looks at it.)*

HARPENDEN *(as she takes the bag)* Nothing. *(nervously)* Just your taxi fare home.

MABEL *(pause while she examines the cheque)* My God! Darling, you are a bloody fool! *(She folds it up deliberately.)* The correct thing for me to do now, I suppose, is to tear it up, grind the pieces into the carpet with my heel, burst into tears and say you've insulted me.

HARPENDEN I hope you don't.

MABEL No, I won't. *(She puts her bag on the phone table.)* It's the sort of insult I appreciate. Those noughts make me dizzy.

HARPENDEN Don't spend it all at once.

MABEL *(musingly)* No. I'll pay a quarter's rent in advance, I'll pay my dentist's bill – he'll have a stroke, poor little man – I'll pay that swine Bojo Sprott back every cent I owe him, plus interest – I'll buy that mink coat – pay for the gin – buy that sapphire brooch – and pay for Brenda's operation. Oh, and what's left can go into War Savings! *(putting the cheque into the bag)* Darling, take that smirk off your face, and don't make any of those nasty dry comments. Will you believe me that there's never been any derrière pensée...

HARPENDEN No, darling, arrière pensée.

MABEL Arrière pensée, then. There's never been any thought of things like this behind any little favours I may have done you in the past. My greed got the better of me just now – otherwise I *would* have torn up that cheque and made a scene. Do you believe me?

HARPENDEN Yes, darling, I do.

MABEL *(going to him)* That's all – except well – goodbye.

He kisses her.

Thank you very much. *(She turns away and wipes her eyes. Trying to laugh)* I've got something in my eye again.

HARPENDEN *(crossing to her)* I'll kiss it well.

The doorbell rings.

Oh, Lord! Now who on earth's that?

MABEL You don't suppose it's Elizabeth – do you?

HARPENDEN I'm pretty sure it's not. She wouldn't come round here alone at this time of night.

MABEL Why ever not?

HARPENDEN She's rather – old-fashioned – in these matters.

The doorbell rings again – twice.

Horton's in bed. Just in case of accident, would you mind awfully going up to the kitchen for a moment?

MABEL Why the kitchen?

HARPENDEN Well, it's the only other room available.

MABEL All right, darling.

HARPENDEN Take your drink. Have you got enough cigarettes?

MABEL *nods.*

Good. *(He pushes her towards the door up left.)* Now go upstairs and turn to the left, not the right – there's where Horton sleeps. *(He picks up a paper off the drinks table.)* Here's the *New Statesman.* *(He hands it to her.)* Or would you rather I sent you up a man to keep you company?

MABEL Which do you think?

She goes out, leaving him with the New Statesman.

The doorbell rings again – three times.

HARPENDEN *(shouting)* Joe! *(He opens the bedroom door.)* Joe, Joe! Come out of there.

MULVANEY *(coming out of the bedroom – his tie and collar undone)* What's cooking?

HARPENDEN That's exactly it. You're to go up to the kitchen, and keep Mabel Crum company.

MULVANEY The kitchen? Why? What are we going to do up there?

HARPENDEN Do you want me to brief you? Here, take this bottle of gin. *(pushing him towards the hall door)* Up the stairs and turn to the left.

MULVANEY *allows himself to be pushed out.* HARPENDEN *follows him. After a second we hear his voice in the hall.*

(offstage) I'm sorry, sir. I had no idea...

DUKE *(offstage)* That's all right, my boy.

The DUKE *enters, followed by* HARPENDEN, *who shuts the door. The* DUKE *crosses right below the settee.* HARPENDEN *follows him to centre.*

I had to see you. It's most urgent. If you hadn't been in I'd have camped on your doorstep all night.

HARPENDEN *(patiently)* Yes, sir. As a matter of fact, I should have rung you up about it. I went to see my solicitors this afternoon...

DUKE *(testily)* What the devil are you talking about?

HARPENDEN The marriage settlement, sir. I've had them insert that clause you wanted.

DUKE Oh, you did? Well, that was extremely good of you, my boy.

HARPENDEN Not at all, sir.

DUKE *(explosively)* Damnation!

HARPENDEN *(startled)* I beg your pardon?

DUKE My boy, are you feeling strong enough to stand a shock?

HARPENDEN Yes – I think so, sir – why?

DUKE I've just come from seeing Elizabeth. I was with her for over four hours, but she's adamant, I'm afraid – adamant.

HARPENDEN Adamant about what?

DUKE My boy – brace yourself.

HARPENDEN Yes, sir. I have braced myself.

DUKE She says she's not going to marry you.

HARPENDEN *(after a pause)* Oh!

DUKE *(testily)* Did you hear what I said?

HARPENDEN Yes. I heard what you said. Why isn't she going to marry me?

DUKE *(sitting on the settee)* That's just it. I don't know.

HARPENDEN Oh!

DUKE She talked a lot of gibberish about planned alliance and wrecking two lives and your not having any white-hot burning thingamagig about you, or something...

HARPENDEN *(leaning down to the* **DUKE***)* What was that you said about white-hot burning thingamagig?

DUKE Well, I can't remember the words exactly, but there was something about a voluptuous flame, and then there was this white-hot burning poppycock. Well, to cut a long story short she says she's not in love with you any more.

HARPENDEN Oh!

DUKE *(testily)* Don't keep standing there saying "Oh".

HARPENDEN There doesn't seem much else to say, except "Oh".

DUKE *(rising)* Good God, man! You're not going to leave it at that, are you?

HARPENDEN Well, if she feels she doesn't love me...

DUKE *(shocked)* Good Lord! I'm amazed at you, Robert, my boy. *(going to him)* I really am. Why, if I were in your shoes, do you know what I'd do?

HARPENDEN No, sir. What?

DUKE I'd raise heaven and earth to make her change her mind. I'd kick up such a shindy they'd hear me in Timbuctoo.

He moves down right.

HARPENDEN *(moving towards him)* You suggest that I should stand outside Brown's Hotel and make a disturbance?

DUKE *(impatiently)* No, no, no. *(crossing back to him)* You misunderstand me. I mean storm her, woo her, take her by force.

HARPENDEN That's not quite my line, I'm afraid.

DUKE Good Lord! I thought you were a man.

HARPENDEN What's your definition of a man, Duke?

DUKE Someone who *does* something at a moment like this, instead of just standing there, wilting like a swooning lily.

HARPENDEN Who's wilting like a swooning lily?

DUKE You are. Why, good Lord, man, look at you...

HARPENDEN I take it, sir, that in spite of the fact your daughter says she doesn't love me, you're still in favour of this match.

DUKE Of course I'm in favour of this match – it's a damned good match. *(He goes to* HARPENDEN *and puts his arm round his shoulders.)* You know, my boy, I'm fond of you, you know that. I feel about you as I'd feel about my own son.

HARPENDEN Thank you, sir.

DUKE Well – what are you going to do about it, eh?

HARPENDEN *(turning left)* I'm going to have a drink. *(He goes to the drinks table.)*

DUKE Robert, I'm disappointed in you. *(He sits on the settee.)*

HARPENDEN *(pouring a drink)* Anything for you?

DUKE I'll have a pint of Pomeroy. Got any Pomeroy?

HARPENDEN No.

DUKE Whisky and soda.

HARPENDEN *(bringing drinks to the* DUKE*)* What on earth made her change her mind like this?

DUKE Well, I've been thinking it out and it occurred to me that something that happened this morning might have some connection... *(taking a drink from* HARPENDEN. *Automatically)* Good health!

HARPENDEN *(sitting on the stool centre, and drinking)* What happened this morning?

DUKE Something devilish fishy. Deuced odd, the whole thing. After I'd dropped you at the Admiralty... By the way, I suppose there was no trouble about your being late, was there?

HARPENDEN There was, but it doesn't matter.

DUKE Sorry, my boy, I'll ring up the First Lord to-morrow. What's his name...socialist wallah...

HARPENDEN Alexander...but for God's sake don't. Go on. What was this fishy thing that happened?

DUKE Well, I came back here to pick up Elizabeth and I found her in a state I can only describe as peculiar.

HARPENDEN Peculiar? How peculiar?

DUKE Devilish peculiar. Between you and me, my boy, and don't let it go any further – if it hadn't been Elizabeth I'd have said she was sozzled.

HARPENDEN Sozzled? Elizabeth—

DUKE Stinko – profundo.

HARPENDEN I don't believe it.

DUKE She insisted on putting her feet up on the sofa and dropping off to sleep, there and then.

HARPENDEN Well, she had a headache. She told me so when she put me off for lunch.

DUKE *(darkly)* Yes. Later on she did have a headache. Not at the time though. She was as gay as a bee, when I found her. *(in a confidential whisper)* And her breath!

HARPENDEN Sherry?

DUKE Whisky.

HARPENDEN But she hates whisky.

DUKE My boy – it was unmistakable. *(He drinks.)* You can't fool me. I've had too much experience of it in our family. *(He drinks.)*

HARPENDEN Good Lord!

DUKE But that's not the end of it. Just before I came into the sitting room, while I was talking to Horton out in the hall, a young fella came dashing past me and out through the front door, going like the wind.

HARPENDEN Who was it?

DUKE Never clapped eyes on him in all my life.

HARPENDEN Did Elizabeth know who he was?

DUKE Well, I asked her and she said – and this is what made me suspicious – she said he'd dropped from the skies. At first I thought she meant one of those parachutist fellows.

HARPENDEN What did he look like?

DUKE Well, he was tall and dark – and he was in uniform – not our uniform – as a matter of fact, I think he might have been one of those Americans who are wandering around all over London these days.

HARPENDEN An American! *(rising)* I know who it is!

DUKE You do? Right, my boy, your duty is plain. *(He rises.)* You must get in touch with this scallywag...

HARPENDEN I don't need to get in touch with him. I mean he's here.

DUKE Here? Where?

HARPENDEN In the kitchen.

DUKE What's he doing there?

HARPENDEN I tremble to think.

DUKE *(crossing up left)* Well, good Lord, don't just stand there, get him down from the kitchen.

HARPENDEN *(doubtfully)* Well, I'm not at all sure—

DUKE Well, *(He puts his glass on the drinks table.)* if you won't I will. *(He opens the door left, and yells up)* Hey, you! Up in the kitchen – whoever you are. Leave whatever you're doing and come down at once! At once, do you understand? *(He shuts the door, and crosses down right.)*

HARPENDEN What am I to say to him?

DUKE Leave it to me.

MULVANEY enters up left, followed by MABEL.

Now, sir... *(He sees MABEL.)* What is this woman doing here?

MABEL *(brightly – to the DUKE, crossing to him, right)* Hullo, Tibby, darling.

DUKE Oh, it's you, Mabs. *(He gives her a quick peck. She sits at the left end of the settee.)* Now, sir, I must ask you to explain yourself...

He addresses MULVANEY, who has moved down left centre.

HARPENDEN *(pacifically)* By the way, this is Lieutenant Mulvaney – the Duke of Ayr and Stirling.

MULVANEY Holy Mackerel! A duke!

DUKE I want a straight answer to a straight question. Have you or have you not been making love to my daughter?

MULVANEY *(after a pause)* Well, here's the way it is – your – by the way, what do I call you?

DUKE Never mind what you call me. Answer my question.

MULVANEY *(to* HARPENDEN*)* Is the Duke of Ayr and Whosis your father-in-law?

HARPENDEN Yes – to be – or rather – not to be.

MABEL Oh darling, what a lovely Hamlet you'd make.

DUKE Stop it, Mabel. You oughtn't to be here at all.

HARPENDEN Darling, go back to the kitchen – do you mind?

MABEL Oh, no. Please let me stay. It looks so exciting.

DUKE *(thundering)* Go back to the kitchen, Mabs.

MABEL *(rising)* All right— *(She goes up towards the door left.)* If the Lieutenant did make love to your daughter, you might ask her to get in touch with me sometime.

She exits. HARPENDEN *snatches up the New Statesman and hands it to her through the door.*

HARPENDEN Darling, the *New Statesman.* *(He closes the door.)*

DUKE Now, sir, your answer?

MULVANEY *(crossing to centre)* Well, Duke, I guess the answer is yes – I did make love to your daughter.

HARPENDEN *(moving down left. Hurt)* Joe!

MULVANEY *(turning to* HARPENDEN*)* I'm sorry, Bobby. I should have told you, I guess, but I didn't have the nerve. You see, the whole thing was a ghastly mistake.

DUKE A mistake? You have the confounded impudence to force your attentions on my daughter – after taking good care – mark you – to render her blotto – and then you stand there and tell me it was just a mistake.

MULVANEY But it was a mistake, Duke. You see, I thought your
daughter was...Mabel Crum...

The DUKE *is rendered temporarily speechless.*

HARPENDEN Oh, God! Of course. I see it all now—

DUKE You thought my daughter was Mabel Crum?

HARPENDEN *(crossing to the* DUKE*)* Yes, yes, of course he did.
(turning to MULVANEY*)* It was a perfectly natural thing
for him to do.

DUKE You will forgive me if I cannot see why it should be a
perfectly natural thing for this fellow to think my daughter...

HARPENDEN *(to* MULVANEY*)* Joe, I forgive you for everything,
but whatever it was you said to Elizabeth has had the effect
of making her say she won't marry me—

MULVANEY *(looking more pleased than upset)* It has? Well,
can you beat that?

DUKE *(returning once more to the attack)* I may be very obtuse,
but I must continue to ask why this gentleman thought my
daughter was Mabel Crum.

The doorbell rings.

HARPENDEN Oh, God! Joe, run and see who that is. I'm out
to everybody.

MULVANEY Sure thing! *(He runs out into the hall.)*

DUKE You may be satisfied with this feller's explanation, but
it seems devilish fishy to me. What I want to know is, why
on earth should he think my daughter is Mabel Crum?

HARPENDEN For Heaven's sake, he did, sir. Isn't that enough
for you?

DUKE No.

MULVANEY *returns.*

MULVANEY *(at the door)* It's a little French guy. He says that you promised him he could sleep here.

HARPENDEN Where is he?

MULVANEY Right here in the hall.

HARPENDEN *(moving up right centre)* Come in, won't you?

> COLBERT *enters, and walks across to* HARPENDEN, *who shakes hands with him.*

How are you? I'm so glad you came. Nice to see you. *(He starts backing him to the door left.)* I wonder if you'd mind awfully going up to the kitchen for a moment?

COLBERT *(backing up left)* The kitchen?

HARPENDEN *(up left centre)* It's upstairs and turn to the left. You can't miss it.

MULVANEY *(pushing him through the door)* Two armchairs and a bottle of gin.

> COLBERT *by this time is outside the door.*

HARPENDEN And a lady who'll be absolutely delighted to see you.

> MULVANEY *shuts the door, and moves down left centre.* HARPENDEN *moves down centre.*

Now listen, Joe, you've got to put this right.

MULVANEY What do you want me to do, Bobby?

HARPENDEN The best thing, I should think, would be to go round to Brown's and explain the whole thing.

DUKE What's the good of that? He'll only start making love to her again.

HARPENDEN Oh, no, he won't.

MULVANEY *(miserable)* What makes you think I won't?

HARPENDEN *(moving towards him)* Joe!

DUKE *(triumphantly)* There! Did you hear that? The feller's not to be trusted an inch. *(He crosses up behind the settee to centre.)*

HARPENDEN *(appalled)* Joe, you're not serious?

MULVANEY Never more serious in my life, Bobby.

HARPENDEN But – but you've only known her since this morning.

MULVANEY While you've known her all your life. What's the difference?

HARPENDEN *(under his breath as he sinks into the chair left centre)* Good Lord!

MULVANEY I'd never have said a word about this, if Elizabeth hadn't spoken up first.

HARPENDEN You think she feels the same way about you?

MULVANEY Doesn't it look that way to you?

HARPENDEN Yes. I suppose it does. Good heavens!

The **DUKE,** *up right centre, who has been glancing from one to the other in bewilderment, now advances on* **MULVANEY,** *moving down centre.*

DUKE Am I to understand, sir, from all this rigmarole that you are now batting on an entirely different wicket?

MULVANEY *(politely, turning to face the* **DUKE***)* Come again, Duke?

DUKE A moment ago you gave as an explanation for your conduct the fact that you mistook my daughter for an unfortunate lady who shall be nameless. Now as I understand it, you're claiming that your motives are sincere and your intentions are honourable.

MULVANEY Well, Duke – if you want it in plain English, here it is. I think I love your daughter and I think your daughter loves me.

DUKE *(turning away right)* Good God!

MULVANEY Sorry, Bobby. *(moving centre, and turning)* It does seem one hell of a way to return your hospitality.

HARPENDEN Don't start apologizing, for God's sake. I couldn't bear it.

DUKE Oh – so you couldn't bear it. Why, good God, man, you're not going to let him snatch the girl you love from under your very nose?

HARPENDEN How can I stop him?

MULVANEY *moves above the left end of the settee.*

DUKE Well, damn it, you can fight him, can't you? Knock him for six through that window!

HARPENDEN, *sunk deep in the armchair left centre, looks up at* MULVANEY.

HARPENDEN He's too big. Besides, I like him.

DUKE Like him? What's that got to do with it? *(He moves down right.)*

COLBERT *enters up left quietly.*

COLBERT Pardon me, please. *(He crosses to centre.)*

DUKE *(testily)* Go away, Monsieur. Allez-vous-en.

COLBERT Mademoiselle Crum has told me that something has arisen in connection with Milady Elizabeth. Might I ask, is it that Milady has decided not to marry Milord Harpenden?

HARPENDEN Yes. That's right.

COLBERT Then if you are searching for the reason of her decision I think I can give it to you. It is I alone who am responsible.

DUKE What?

HARPENDEN *sits up a little.*

COLBERT This morning I advised the Lady Elizabeth not to marry this Lord.

DUKE Wait a minute. *(He goes towards him.)* Am I to understand that you made love to my daughter too this morning?

COLBERT I cannot deny it, Monsieur.

DUKE But why, Monsieur? *Pourquoi?* I suppose you thought she was Mistinguette?

COLBERT No, Monsieur. Because I love her.

There is a moment's pause, while everyone stares at **COLBERT** *wonderingly.*

What is more, Monsieur, if, as you say, your daughter has taken my advice, then it appears probable that she has returned my love.

Another pause.

DUKE I shall be obliged, gentlemen, if, when in due course you have concluded your deliberations, you would inform me with how many members of the United Nations my daughter is to form an attachment? *(He crosses up left, between* **MULVANEY** *and* **COLBERT**, *and turns at the door.)* Personally, I'm going up to the kitchen to have a gin with Mabel Cram.

He exits.

There is a pause, while **HARPENDEN** *and* **MULVANEY** *stare, bewildered, at* **COLBERT**.

COLBERT *(with quiet martyrdom, moving down right)* I suppose you will wish to knock me down, Milord.

HARPENDEN *(rising)* You're certainly smaller than he is – but at the moment I don't see what's to be gained by knocking you down either.

MULVANEY *(moving quickly down towards* **COLBERT**) Considerable satisfaction.

HARPENDEN *(restraining him)* Wait a minute, Joe. Don't let's start a rough house yet. If you fight him, then I've got to fight you – and after he's recovered I've got to fight him again. Now that's too much fighting for one night. Let's try a little international arbitration first.

MULVANEY (*crossing* HARPENDEN *to down left centre*) Aw, hell, Bobby, there's no sense in arbitrating with this guy. He's screwy. (*turning to face* HARPENDEN) He doesn't know what he's talking about. Let's you and me gang up on him and bounce him down the stairs – what do you say?

COLBERT Tiens! I see I am facing two enemies. That is a surprise. (*to* MULVANEY, *moving up right centre*) I should have thought you would have been my ally, seeing that my confession has saved you from being falsely accused of stealing this lord's fiancée.

MULVANEY (*hotly*) Falsely accused nothing! Elizabeth is leaving Bobby because of me – see?

COLBERT I don't think so, Monsieur. She is leaving him because of me.

HARPENDEN *stands between them, watching with raised eyebrows.*

MULVANEY (*belligerently*) Listen, I made love to her.

COLBERT So did I make love to her.

MULVANEY I said she was the loveliest thing I ever saw in all my life.

COLBERT I too said she was very beautiful.

MULVANEY Yeah – but I made real love to her – see. (*He pauses.*) *I* kissed her.

COLBERT *stares at* MULVANEY. HARPENDEN *bows to* COLBERT.

HARPENDEN (*politely*) Go on, Monsieur. Don't let it rest at that. Tell him what you did to my fiancée.

MULVANEY *(contrite)* Aw, say, listen, Bobby, I'm terribly sorry – but this guy's got me all balled up.

COLBERT *(to* MULVANEY*)* At what hour did you take these liberties with Milord's fiancée?

MULVANEY What the hell does it matter what hour? *(He moves down left.)*

COLBERT It matters very much. *(following him)* Try – if you will, to remember – was it after eleven o'clock?

MULVANEY Not much after.

COLBERT But after, none the less?

MULVANEY Yeah, I guess so.

COLBERT What abominable luck! *(crossing right)* Sacré nom d'une pipe! *(turning)* And these attentions of yours – she repaid them?

MULVANEY I'll say she did. *(as an afterthought)* I'm sorry, Bobby.

HARPENDEN *(ironically)* Not at all. Just imagine I'm not here. Personally I'm going to curl up on the sofa with a good book. *(He sits down on the settee and takes a book from the table behind it, opens it, and pretends to read.)*

COLBERT I too am most sorry, Milord, to be forced to say such things before you.

HARPENDEN Don't worry about me. *(He takes his book up and then lowers it again.)* Oh, before you go on – I think I ought to tell you – I hope you both won't be too angry with me – this morning I too made a little love to my fiancée ; and at one moment I even went so far as to give her a kiss. I'm most terribly sorry. You must both try to be generous and forgive me. *(He puts his legs up on the settee, facing right, and starts to read.)*

COLBERT *(sitting at the right end of the settee)* At what hour did you give your fiancée a kiss, Milord?

HARPENDEN Oh, yes, of course, that's very important, isn't it ? It was – let me see – about ten minutes to eleven.

COLBERT Ten minutes to eleven? That is all right, then. It was a few minutes after eleven that I advised her not to marry you and to await a lover more worthy of her.

HARPENDEN Oh, I see. A lover more worthy of her?

COLBERT Yes, Milord. I was naturally referring to myself and had too much delicacy to say so; but I'm afraid that it looks now as if she might have made the ludicrous error of applying my advice to this lieutenant.

HARPENDEN (*rising*) I'm terribly sorry – you haven't been introduced, have you? This is lieutenant Mulvaney – Lieutenant Colbert.

COLBERT *rises, moves centre, and holds out his hand.* MULVANEY *crosses to him, slaps his hand into the air, and crosses him to right of the settee.*

MULVANEY (*as he crosses*) Aw nuts! (*turning at right*) Listen, you. What right have you got to go dashing about saying those sort of things to guys' fiancées?

HARPENDEN (*from the settee*) Ha!

MULVANEY (*to* HARPENDEN) Well, at least I had some sort of excuse for behaving as I did. He had none.

COLBERT (*at centre*) I had every excuse. Last night, on the train from Inverness to London, I sat next to the most adorable young girl I have yet seen in England. She is merely Corporal W.A.A.F., so naturally I open conversation.

MULVANEY You see the sort of guy this is – a railroad menace.

COLBERT Not at all. (*moving left*) When in Rome I do as the Romans, and in English trains I usually try to give the impression of having died in my seat. (*He crosses back to the stool left of the settee, and sits.*) But this opportunity I could not let to pass. I find my WAAF is not at all what I imagined. She speaks to me in perfect French and before long we are telling each other the most intimate details of our private lives. I find she is to marry the following day a young and immensely rich noble whom she patently – from a thousand little hints she gives me – does not love and who, it is equally patent, does not love her.

HARPENDEN *(sitting up, aggressively)* And why is that so patent?

COLBERT I find he keeps a mistress.

HARPENDEN I keep a mistress?

COLBERT That young lady I have just met in the kitchen – is she not a mistress?

HARPENDEN No. She's Mabel Crum. *(He lies back again.)*

COLBERT Do not misunderstand me, Milord. I am not prudish in these matters. A man can keep a hundred mistresses and still maintain a happy and successful marriage. But when I hear that he keeps a Mabel Crum – naturally I say – then of course he cannot love Elizabeth as wholeheartedly, as devotedly, with the same white-hot burning passion...

HARPENDEN *(slamming the book down, and sitting up)* Aha! White-hot burning thingammy, eh?

COLBERT My lord?

HARPENDEN She mentioned some such idiotic phrase to her father when she told him she wasn't going to marry me.

COLBERT *(rising)* She did? Splendid! Then perhaps it is still possible she has returned my passion. C'est épatant. *(moving upstage centre)*

MULVANEY *(moving up to him behind the settee)* Listen, you little rat, the only way she'd return your passion is through the mail marked "Not wanted".

COLBERT The situation is not helped by impoliteness, Monsieur. We are at an impasse. You maintain she loves you, I maintain she loves me. We must devise a scheme of finding out the truth.

HARPENDEN *has been thinking during these last few lines, now he slaps his knee and crosses quickly to the armchair left centre, and takes up the receiver. When they see this,* COLBERT *moves down left, and* MULVANEY *to centre, beside the phone table.*

MULVANEY Good for you, Bobby – only, say, listen – let me talk to her, will you?

COLBERT If he talks to her it is only fair play I talk to her too.

HARPENDEN *(replacing the receiver)* Look, I am a patient man. I have sat – mainly in silence – while you two gentlemen have gloatingly described in the fullest and most sordid details the vile attentions you have forced upon the girl I love. May I remind you both, however, that you are under my roof, and you're both very much mistaken if either of you imagines that you're going to have twopence worth of verbal loveplay with my fiancée on my telephone. *(He starts dialling again.)*

The others watch the number he dials.

COLBERT *(when* HARPENDEN *has dialled)* But – Milord – since this evening she is no longer your fiancée.

HARPENDEN We'll see about that. *(into the phone)* Hullo – Brown's? Lady Elizabeth Randall, please... Yes, darling. Bobby... No, please don't... All right, then. I promise not to argue. Just tell me why – I'm surely entitled to know that... Yes, but your father wasn't as explicit as I'd like and... When will I get it? ...To-morrow? Yes, but I want to know tonight... Darling, don't cry... I only want to know what's happened... Why can't you? ...Yes, but what's the difference between loving someone and being in love with someone?

COLBERT *gestures and mutters to himself.*

All right then, tell me. Is there someone else? ...What do you mean, you don't know? ...Well, let me tell you, I do know...

MULVANEY *makes a grab for the receiver, but* HARPENDEN *changes it to his left ear.*

Yes, I know more about it than you think. I know it's one of two men—

COLBERT *(urgently, grabbing for the receiver)* The fair play, Milord.

HARPENDEN *(moving the receiver back to his right ear and speaking into it)* The fair play, my fanny! *(He covers the mouthpiece with his hand, looks worried and then speaks into it again.)* Sorry, darling... All right, well, let me tell you – so that you'll be warned. One of them is a vicious French snake who goes about bothering young WAAFs in railway carriages, and the other is a lecherous American who mistook you for a trollop!

MULVANEY Hey – you little rat! *(He tries to get the receiver, but is again thwarted. Shouting :)* Don't believe him, Elizabeth...

HARPENDEN No, darling, I don't hear anything, crossed line, I expect... Yes, darling. A trollop... Well, apparently he expected to find a trollop in my sitting room... *(crossly)* No, I don't know why... Well, you know what these Americans are, they expect to find trollops wherever they go... Darling, be reasonable...

MULVANEY *(grabbing, and getting the receiver this time)* It's not true, Elizabeth, I don't think you're a trollop – I love you.

COLBERT *(getting the receiver from* MULVANEY*)* I am not a vicious French snake – and I love you passionately, devotedly, with a burning... *(He shrugs his shoulders.)* She has rung off. *(He "puts the receiver on* HARPENDEN*'s knee, and moves down left)*

HARPENDEN What did you expect?

COLBERT *(turning, at left)* Milord, I am simply astonished with you. Was that what you learned on the playing fields of Eton?

HARPENDEN I was at Harrow.

MULVANEY *(displaying an enormous fist)* I've a good mind to punch you right on the nose!

HARPENDEN Really! This display of righteous indignation comes a little oddly from you two gentlemen, I must say. Must I remind you both that I have known and loved Elizabeth for some twenty years – while you two—

COLBERT Pa – fambleu, so what!

HARPENDEN I beg your pardon?

COLBERT The world is no longer what it was when this match between you and Elizabeth was first planned. Les droits de seigneur have gone – never to return. You are a doomed class.

HARPENDEN All right. *(He rises, crosses to the settee, and sits.)* I'm a doomed class, but that's no reason I shouldn't marry the girl I love, is it?

COLBERT Certainly it is if that girl is Elizabeth. *(He crosses to him.)* At all costs she must be saved from sharing your doom.

HARPENDEN Left wing, eh?

COLBERT Socialiste.

HARPENDEN Well, I read the *New Statesman* myself.

COLBERT That will not save you from extinction.

MULVANEY, *who during all this has been thinking how to get out, makes a furtive move towards the door, putting on his hat.* HARPENDEN *sees him and jumps up.*

HARPENDEN *(sharply – crossing to him up left)* Hey! where do you think you're going?

MULVANEY Oh, I just thought I'd go out for a little stroll.

HARPENDEN I suppose your stroll wouldn't take you anywhere near Brown's Hotel, would it?

MULVANEY I don't even know where Brown's Hotel is.

HARPENDEN Then of course you wouldn't think of asking a policeman, would you? *(He gets between* MULVANEY *and the door left.)* No, you don't go for a little stroll. You're not leaving this flat tonight.

MULVANEY How do you think you're going to stop me?

HARPENDEN I don't know – but I'm going to have a good try.

COLBERT *(crossing to* MULVANEY*)* If you attack Milord I shall assist him.

MULVANEY I'm quite ready to take on the two of you.

COLBERT Without doubt, but have you forgotten that we are guests in Milord's flat?

MULVANEY There's no reason why he should keep me locked in here all night like a little boy. If I want to go for a stroll, why shouldn't I go for a stroll? I'm a free man, aren't I?

HARPENDEN If you want exercise I've got a rowing machine in my bathroom.

MULVANEY Oh, Bobby, but you don't want to break the poor girl's heart, do you? *(He breaks away, goes to the settee, and sits.)* She loves me, God damn it!

COLBERT *(crossing to the settee, and tapping* MULVANEY *on the shoulder)* That fact is not yet fully established, Monsieur. *(He crosses to the chair left centre, and sits)* It may well be myself she loves.

HARPENDEN *(moving to the settee, and sitting at the right end)* You both seem to forget that several hours have passed since eleven o'clock this morning. All sorts of Poles, Czechs, Belgians and Dutchmen may have made love to her since then – or she may have gone dotty about the night porter at Brown's.

MULVANEY *(pleadingly)* Look, Bobby, be reasonable, will you? I got to get to see Elizabeth tonight.

COLBERT If he goes, then I go too.

HARPENDEN And if you both go, I go with you.

COLBERT Another impasse. There is only one solution.

HARPENDEN What's that? The fair play?

COLBERT Exactly, Milord – the fair play. Each man to go round to Brown's Hotel in turn.

MULVANEY Yeah – who goes first?

COLBERT *(brightly)* Alphabetical order?

MULVANEY No, thank you, Mr. Colbert.

COLBERT Then we must toss up a coin.

HARPENDEN Hey, wait a minute. I don't think I agree to this.

COLBERT Where is your spirit of sport, Milord?

HARPENDEN Buried on the playing fields of Harrow.

COLBERT If you do not agree to my suggestion, Milord, then I shall be painfully compelled to side with this large lieutenant against you. You would not then stand much chance.

MULVANEY I got an idea. *(He rises, and moves to centre.)* Do you guys play craps? *(He gets dice out of his pocket.)*

COLBERT Once – a long time ago. I have forgotten.

MULVANEY Well, it's quite simple. Do you know how, Bobby?

HARPENDEN *(sulkily)* Yes, vaguely. You have to make seven, or something, don't you?

MULVANEY *(kneeling at centre)* Yeah. A seven or eleven wins straight off – two or three loses. But with anything else – say a six or an eight, you have to throw until you make that number – when you'd win – or a seven – when you'd lose. Get the idea?

COLBERT I think so, yes.

MULVANEY *(to* HARPENDEN*)* Ok, Bobby. I'll play you first.

HARPENDEN *kneels on the floor, left of* MULVANEY.

Now you take one and flip it!

HARPENDEN Flip it?

MULVANEY Like that. *(He demonstrates.)* Ok. Mine! I shoot first. *(He rolls the dice.)* Eight. Now I got to throw an eight before I throw a seven.

The DUKE *enters up left, unnoticed, and watches them.*

(chanting) Little eighter from decatur! Little eighter sweet potater! Come up for Daddy! *(He throws again.)*

DUKE I trust you're all enjoying yourselves? *(He crosses to centre.)*

COLBERT Yes, thank you, Monsieur. *(He kneels left of* MULVANEY.*)*

DUKE May I ask what you're doing?

MULVANEY Shooting craps, Duke.

DUKE *(icily)* I gather you've settled to your mutual satisfaction the unimportant little problem on which you were engaged when I left you.

HARPENDEN Well – in a sense – this game is going to settle that.

MULVANEY *(chanting)* Come up, little five and three – come up, little four and four.

DUKE *(outraged)* What? Do you mean to tell me you're playing craps for my daughter?

COLBERT *(rising)* We are playing to decide who proposes to her first.

DUKE *(thundering)* But this is monstrous, it's unheard of. It's eighteenth century. *(taking a step forward)* Stop this obscenity at once!

MULVANEY Clear the floor, will you, Duke, you're spoiling my throw. *(He throws.)* There she is, four and four. Ok, Frenchy. Now it's you and me. Take one and flip it.

DUKE *(aghast)* Well, would you believe it!

COLBERT, *paying no attention to the* DUKE, *flips a single dice.*

MULVANEY Ok. That's your throw.

DUKE *(roaring)* May I remind you gentlemen that it's my daughter you're dicing for?

COLBERT *(throws)* Nine. Is that good?

MULVANEY Not very. Can win, though. Try and throw another four and five, or six and three.

COLBERT That won't be easy. *(He throws.)*

The DUKE *comes forward and watches.*

Four. *(He throws again.)* Eight. That's nearer.

MULVANEY It's near a seven too.

COLBERT *(throws)* Ten. Zut!

DUKE He has to throw a nine before he throws a seven, is that it?

MULVANEY That's it, Duke.

DUKE Poor old Chicken Hartopp lost a fortune at this game at Miami.

MULVANEY He's not the first sucker who's done that, Duke.

DUKE *(kneeling beside them centre)* You know, I haven't played craps for years!

COLBERT *throws again as—*

The curtain falls.

ACT III

Scene One

Scene. The same.

Time. About 3 a.m. the following morning.

When the curtain rises, **COLBERT** *is asleep in the armchair left centre. The* **DUKE,** *sitting on a cushion on the floor, below the right end of the settee, is throwing dice.* **HARPENDEN,** *sitting on the floor, left of the* **DUKE,** *is watching him dourly. Both are holding glasses of whisky.*

DUKE Come up, little four and two, come up for papa. *(He throws again.)* There she is. There's my beauty. Six it is. *(He adds something to a much scribbled-on score sheet, humming in high good humour.)* That makes you owe me – let me see – now – five hundred and sixty-five pounds ten shillings – do you agree?

HARPENDEN *(glumly)* If you say so.

DUKE My good child, have a look at the sheet. *(He waves it at him.)*

HARPENDEN That's all right. I can't add, anyway. *(He finishes his drink and rises.)*

DUKE *(chuckling)* Can't add, my boy? No wonder they won't give you a commission. *(He finishes his drink and holds out his glass.)* Here – you might get me one too while you're about it.

HARPENDEN *takes his glass, and with his own goes to the drinks table.*

Now this time I think I'll put up a pony. *(He glances at the score sheet.)* Twenty-five pounds, are you on?

HARPENDEN All right – but don't shoot till I get back.

DUKE My dear boy – what do you think I am?

HARPENDEN *opens his mouth to tell him, but decides against it.* COLBERT *looks up at* HARPENDEN.

COLBERT Still not returned?

HARPENDEN No. *(He consults his watch.)* He's now been gone three hours and fifty minutes.

COLBERT *(unmoved)* It is nothing. Possibly she will not see him and he is still waiting in the hall of the hotel.

HARPENDEN *(gloomily)* Not Joe. He's the type who breaks down doors and things.

COLBERT *(hopefully)* Then possibly he is in prison?

HARPENDEN That's too much to hope for.

DUKE *(testily)* Don't stand there chattering. I've got a pony in the pot.

HARPENDEN *(crossing back to the* DUKE, *handing him a glass)* We were discussing the trivial little matter of your daughter's future, sir. *(He sits on the left arm of the settee.)*

DUKE What's that? Oh yes. This feller's not come back yet?

HARPENDEN *shakes his head.*

Oh well – I'll lay three monkeys to one against him.

HARPENDEN I'll take that.

DUKE *(after a slight pause)* How long has he been gone?

HARPENDEN Nearly four hours.

DUKE Hm. Well, I'm afraid, as a father, it's hardly right for me to accept a wager like that. Sorry, old man. Now, there's twenty-five smackers in the bank, and I'm shooting. *(He rolls the dice.)* Seven. Good Lord! *(without conviction)* I hoped you were going to win that time – my boy. *(He adds the score to the sheet.)* Now that makes you owe me six hundred pounds and ten shillings, exactly.

HARPENDEN Just a minute. *(taking the sheet from him)* Five hundred and ninety pounds, ten shillings.

DUKE *(taking back the sleet)* What's that? *(He studies it.)* Yes, that's right. Stupid mistake. What was that about your not being able to add?

*The **DUKE** studies the score sheet again. **HARPENDEN** suddenly pricks up his ears at a noise outside. He darts quickly to the hall.*

Well – Robert – I'll give you a real chance this time. I'm going to put up fifty. *(noticing **HARPENDEN**'s absence)* Where is he?

***HARPENDEN** comes back looking disappointed. **COLBERT** looks at him enquiringly.*

HARPENDEN *(crossing to centre)* People next door.

***COLBERT** nods and prepares to go to sleep again.*

DUKE I was saying, Robert, I'm going to give you a real chance this time and...

HARPENDEN *(shortly, crossing left to right upstage)* Thank you, sir, but I'm not playing any more.

DUKE But, my boy, I've won too much money off you. You'd better let me give you a few more rolls.

HARPENDEN It's very kind of you, sir, but I'd far rather you didn't give me even one more roll.

DUKE It's for your own good.

HARPENDEN I'm quite aware of that, sir – but I'm prepared to make that sacrifice.

DUKE Oh, very well – if you really don't want to play any more – I must say I feel very uncomfortable having won all this money off you. That'll be – let me see now— *(He studies the score sheet.)* five hundred and ninety pounds, ten shillings. *(magnanimously)* Let's wipe out the ten shillings, shall we?

HARPENDEN No, sir. Thank you all the same.

DUKE *(rising and putting the glass on the table behind the settee)* I feel devilish tired. *(He sees the clock on the desk.)* Good Lord, four o'clock, no wonder. *(testily)* What's this damned Yankee Doodle mean keeping my daughter out all night?

HARPENDEN The question is not so much what does the damn Yankee Doodle mean, as what does your daughter mean.

DUKE It couldn't take her four hours to send this fellow packing. *(turning on* **HARPENDEN***)* It's all your fault, Robert. You should never have countenanced this diabolical scheme.

HARPENDEN No, sir.

DUKE Why don't you ring up Brown's again instead of just standing there...

HARPENDEN Wilting like a swooning lily?

DUKE Exactly.

HARPENDEN I'm not going to ring up Brown's again for the simple reason that, not fifteen minutes ago, when you were fully absorbed in trying to discover how you had come to cheat yourself of ten shillings on the score, I rang up Brown's for the fourth time since one o'clock.

DUKE *(in kindly tones)* Bit overwrought, aren't you, old man?

HARPENDEN Yes, sir.

DUKE Thought so. Know the signs well. As a matter of fact I remember your ringing now. What did they say?

HARPENDEN That Lady Elizabeth left shortly before twelve with an American gentleman and has not yet returned.

DUKE Damned impertinence. I suppose he's taken her to one of those bottle party places, the Jubilee or somewhere.

HARPENDEN My own guess is Hyde Park.

DUKE *(appalled)* Hyde Park? At four o'clock in the morning! If you think that, why don't you go and look for them in Hyde Park?

HARPENDEN How? With a torch?

DUKE Yes, of course, with a torch.

HARPENDEN I should be lynched for one thing. Besides, Hyde Park is a very big place, and anyway it might be Green Park.

DUKE Yes, or St James's, if it comes to that, with those damned ducks. Well, there's nothing for it but to wait for this feller to come back, I suppose. I'll go and lie down on your bed for a bit, I think. All right? *(He moves up centre.)*

HARPENDEN All right.

DUKE *(pausing on his way)* Quite sure you wouldn't care for...?

HARPENDEN *(firmly)* Yes, sir. Quite sure.

DUKE *(to* COLBERT*)* What about you, Monsieur?

COLBERT *(raises himself on his elbow)* Pardon, Monsieur?

DUKE Voulez-vous rouler avec moi un peu?

COLBERT Comment?

HARPENDEN It's all right. The Duke wants to know if you'd like to throw dice with him.

The **DUKE** *whispers to* **HARPENDEN** *asking what* **COLBERT** *thought he meant.* **HARPENDEN** *whispers back. The* **DUKE** *moves right.*

COLBERT Ah, I see. Thank you, Monsieur, but I never gamble, I'm afraid.

DUKE You don't, eh? I noticed you had no qualms about gambling for my daughter.

COLBERT For such a stake I would gamble all I had in the world.

DUKE And exactly how much is that, if I might ask?

COLBERT In money about twenty pounds.

DUKE Twenty pounds. Quite so, Monsieur. *(with dignity)* I hardly think we need say any more.

He goes into the bedroom.

COLBERT He is quaint, the Duke. He is not, I imagine, typical of all your dukes?

HARPENDEN *(sitting centre of the settee)* You imagine right.

COLBERT You do not think by any chance he is the Duke whom Hess came to see?

HARPENDEN If he is, then Hess by now is almost certainly the holder of a considerable stock in Zippy-Snaps.

COLBERT What are Zippy-Snaps?

HARPENDEN An invention the Duke is interested in. *(He glares at* COLBERT, *malevolently.)* It's an excellent scheme as a matter of fact. *(He rises and crosses to centre.)* Absolutely sure-fire money-maker. You ought to put your twenty pounds into it.

COLBERT My friend, you should not bear *me* a grudge, we must acknowledge that America has conquered us.

HARPENDEN I'm damned if I will.

COLBERT *(sighing)* They say it is a virtue in Englishmen not to know when they are beaten. In this case I would call it ridiculous bravado.

A pause. HARPENDEN *continues to stride back and forwards across the stage behind* COLBERT.

Stop being a tiger in a cage. You make me nervous.

HARPENDEN Good. *(He continues his walking.)*

COLBERT Why are you in such, a state? You don't really love her...

HARPENDEN *(going to him)* Now look here, you've been saying that all the evening. If you say it once more I shall be forced to take steps.

COLBERT What steps?

HARPENDEN I'm wearing regulation boots. *(He displays one.)* I do love her, damn it! *(He sits on the settee.)*

COLBERT And the woman Crum?

HARPENDEN It may interest you to know that after our marriage I'd arranged never to see the woman Crum again.

COLBERT Tiens. *(ruminatively)* As a matter of fact it is among such women that you should choose not only your mistress but your wife.

HARPENDEN Why, may I ask?

COLBERT You will need a simple hard-working girl to look after you – as a mother looks after a child. But the Lady Elizabeth, as it would now appear, is incapable even of looking after herself.

HARPENDEN Why should I need looking after more than anyone else?

COLBERT *(rising and crossing to* HARPENDEN*)* My good friend, imagine yourself when your millions are removed from you, as they will be. Look at you now – a simple sailor. Why do you think you have not yet been made an officer?

HARPENDEN Mere class prejudice. I went to a public school.

COLBERT In the post-war world...

HARPENDEN Now don't go on about my being doomed, it's beginning to depress me. Surely I'd get a pound a week from Sir William Beveridge? *(He rises, moves to the window, opens the curtains slightly and looks out.)* The searchlights have suddenly come on. Perhaps the sirens will go in a minute. *(He moves centre above the settee.)*

COLBERT *(moving to the chair left centre)* They would not hear them. And the searchlights, crossing and inter-crossing the sky with their delicate tracery, will only make matters worse. *(He sits.)*

HARPENDEN *(violently)* She can't do this to me, damn it!

COLBERT My friend, she has already done it to you.

HARPENDEN *(moving down right)* I refuse to be treated like an old sock. Why should she hurl me into the dustbin just because some rollicking American makes a pass at her? Who the hell does she think she is? *(He crosses back centre.)*

COLBERT Ah! *(He sits up.)* Now this is more the spirit.

HARPENDEN My God! The nerve of it! The night before our wedding! *(He goes to the door and back again to centre, as he speaks.)* No thought for me at all. *(imitating)* I'm not in love with you, Bobby, I love you but I'm not in love with you. Just because she has her head filled with some idiotic, blush-making, sentimental slush by a ridiculous little French pick-up...

COLBERT Bravo! This is magnificent!

HARPENDEN The utter insane selfishness of it. She knows quite well I had to go to my captain and beg him on my knees – on my bended knees mind you – for special leave to get married. She knows quite well – because I wrote to her – how difficult it is for me to get this leave – because of that little trouble over my last forty-eight. On my knees I beg my captain. " Very well, Ordinary Seaman Harpenden," he says, " I'll let you have it this time. But, by God, Ordinary Seaman Harpenden," he says, " if this is another of your damned tricks and you don't come back to me on time and married, I'll bloody well put you in irons, Ordinary Seaman Harpenden," he says. She doesn't think of me tossing and groaning and sobbing in irons, does she? Oh no, oh dear me no! There she is, gallivanting about the park like a Bacchante with some great big beefy brute of a bombardier, while I, her true fiancé, am left alone to face disgrace and degradation – my social life ruined and my naval career blighted, before it has begun!

COLBERT Bravo! Bravo! *(He rises and crosses to him.)* This is a fine rage. Well done, Milord Bobby!

MABEL CRUM *enters left. She looks sleepy and cross.*

MABEL *(crossing to the settee)* What's all this noise about?

HARPENDEN Good Lord! What are you doing here?

MABEL I don't know. I thought perhaps you could tell me.

HARPENDEN *(going down to her)* Do you mean to say you've been up in the kitchen all this time?

MABEL I suppose I must have been. I've only just come to, to hear this extraordinary roaring coming from down here. Are you still rehearsing Hamlet, darling? Oh, my God! *(rubbing her back)* I've slept in some funny places in my time, but never before in a kitchen chair. Never again, come to that.

HARPENDEN Oh Lord! I'm terribly sorry. I'm afraid I clean forgot about you up there. Where does it hurt? *(He massages her back.)*

MABEL No, it's higher up, ducky. That's right.

HARPENDEN Do forgive me, won't you?

MABEL Don't be silly, darling. You've had a lot to cope with tonight, haven't you?

COLBERT *goes to the chair left centre and sits.*

HARPENDEN Rather more than usual, I admit.

MABEL Thank you. That's all right now. Can I get myself another drink?

HARPENDEN Yes, of course, I'll get it. *(He goes to the drinks table.)*

MABEL *(sitting at the left end of the settee)* Is Elizabeth leaving you?

HARPENDEN Looks like it.

MABEL For that? *(indicating COLBERT)*

COLBERT No, for Lieutenant Mulvaney, Mademoiselle.

MABEL That's one better, I suppose, but she still must be cuckoo.

COLBERT Perhaps she is not thinking in terms of pounds, shillings and pence, Mademoiselle.

MABEL *(with sincerity)* I never suggested she was. I mean she's cuckoo because the man she's turned down is ten times more attractive than the man she's turned him down for.

COLBERT Probably you are prejudiced, Mademoiselle...

MABEL I'm never prejudiced about men. My God, look at him—

She points to **HARPENDEN,** *who is coming towards her with her drink.*

What more would any girl want?

HARPENDEN *(behind the left end of the settee)* You just like sailors, that's your trouble.

MABEL Of course I do. Who doesn't? *(taking the drink)* Now, I'll just finish this, then I'll start my long trek home.

HARPENDEN How are you going to get to Kensington at this time of night? We'll never get a taxi for you now.

MABEL That's all right, I can walk.

HARPENDEN No, of course you can't walk.

MABEL Darling, I can't stay here, can I? So what else is there?

HARPENDEN Yes, you can stay here. *(He crosses round to left of the settee.)* Certainly you can stay here. Why should I throw open my chambers to any odious Allied officer who likes to take a crack at pinching my girl, and then turn you, my only real friend, out into the night? You're damn well going to stay here.

MABEL Darling, I'm not going back to that kitchen chair...

HARPENDEN No, of course you're not. I know. You can go in Horton's bed.

MABEL What about Horton?

HARPENDEN Oh, I'll get him out first.

MABEL Darling, of course. I meant, where are you going to put him?

HARPENDEN He can go on the sofa.

COLBERT *(sitting up)* What about myself?

HARPENDEN Hm. Well, there's nothing else for it. You'd better go in there with me. *(He points to the bedroom.)* It hardly looks as if Lieutenant Mulvaney is going to honour me with his company in my bed tonight.

COLBERT I am beginning to learn the meaning of the term gentleman.

HARPENDEN *(to* **MABEL***)* Just a minute. *(He goes towards the bedroom door.)* I'll get you something to sleep in. *(He opens the bedroom door and looks inside.)* His Grace, thank heavens, is in a repulsive-looking coma. *(He goes inside.)*

MABEL He's terribly upset, I suppose, about Elizabeth?

COLBERT Surprisingly so, Mademoiselle.

MABEL Why surprisingly? He's in love with the girl.

HARPENDEN *emerges with a pair of red pyjamas over his arm. He hands them to* **MABEL***.*

HARPENDEN *(kneeling at the left end of the settee)* Mabel, my dear, will you marry me?

MABEL *(gazes at him wonderingly)* Why?

HARPENDEN Because I love you so very much.

MABEL Why else?

HARPENDEN Because we get on very well together, and I think you'd make me a very good wife.

MABEL Yes, darling. Why else?

HARPENDEN Because if I don't marry someone this leave I'm going to get into awful trouble with my captain.

MABEL (laughing) Oh, Bobby, you are heaven! (putting her arms round his neck) You don't really want to marry me. Can't you think of anyone else?

HARPENDEN No. There isn't anyone else.

MABEL With two million and a title you can afford the very best.

HARPENDEN I don't want the very best. I want you. (awkwardly) That's to say... (He turns his head away from her.)

MABEL All right, darling. Don't make it worse.

HARPENDEN I really mean it, you know. I'm asking you to marry me. Of course if you'd rather not—

MABEL Bobby, my precious, no girl in her right senses would turn you down.

HARPENDEN One girl has.

MABEL But she wasn't in her right senses. I am. Still, before I definitely commit you, hadn't you better think hard and see if there really isn't someone you'd rather marry than me?

HARPENDEN All right. (He sits on the floor centre, pondering.)

COLBERT, sitting in the chair, has been watching the scene intently.

(at length) No. There's only Lucy Scott, and she's taller than I am.

MABEL She's an awfully nice girl, though.

HARPENDEN Yes, but I don't think I like her awfully.

MABEL Well, of course, if you don't like her awfully...

HARPENDEN No, there really is only you. Do marry me, please?

MABEL If I say yes, you won't try to back out afterwards, will you?

HARPENDEN No, of course not.

MABEL Whatever happens?

HARPENDEN Whatever happens.

MABEL Promise?

HARPENDEN Promise.

MABEL I don't want to be made what I believe is called the laughing stock of London. All right, Bobby, I'll marry you.

COLBERT *rises from his chair and goes to them.*

COLBERT Permit me to congratulate you both.

HARPENDEN *(rising)* Oh, were you there all the time? I ought to have sent you back to the kitchen.

MABEL *rises.*

COLBERT I am glad you did not. I have never before witnessed an English proposal. I would not have missed it for the world.

HARPENDEN *(to* **MABEL***)* Is he being rude? *(He collects the pyjamas from the settee and goes to the door left during* **MABEL***'s speech.)*

MABEL Yes, of course he is. *(crossing to* **COLBERT***, hotly)* But let me tell you, Monsieur What's-your-name, I've been proposed to by hundreds of Frenchmen in my time, as well as all sorts of Poles, Czechs, Norwegians and the rest, and I'd far rather have an honest, straight-forward English proposal like Bobby's than all the hand-kissing and arm-stroking and "Oh, but Mademoiselle is so intoxicating" stuff that you people hand out. I like to know where I am.

She exits up left, **HARPENDEN** *is about to follow her, picks up the New Statesman, and stops in the doorway.*

HARPENDEN Well, what do you think?

COLBERT In theory it should work out all right.

HARPENDEN And in practice?

COLBERT *(with emotion, going to him)* My dear friend, you have my very, very deepest best wishes.

HARPENDEN Oh! *(He considers for a second.)* Well, anyway, they can't put me in irons now, can they?

He exits. COLBERT *shrugs his shoulders, smiles and goes to the telephone. He dials a number, carefully.*

COLBERT *(into the telephone)* Hullo, Brown's Hotel? ...Has Lady Elizabeth Randall come in yet? ...Not yet! ...No, no message. *(He replaces the receiver.)*

HORTON *enters up left, wearing a woollen dressing gown, looking disgruntled. He crosses to the settee.*

HORTON Good morning, sir.

COLBERT Good morning.

HORTON *picks up the cushion from the floor, places it at the left end of the settee, arranges his rug around himself, and lies down, head left.*

HORTON *(at length)* Goodnight, sir.

COLBERT Good night! Ya – ya-ya ces Anglais! *(He crosses right.)*

There are voices in the hall and ELIZABETH *and* MULVANEY *come in.* ELIZABETH *is now in "civvies". Both are excited, happy and gay.* HORTON *gets up.*

MULVANEY Hullo, there!

COLBERT At last!

ELIZABETH Good morning, Horton.

HORTON Good morning, my Lady.

ELIZABETH Sorry if we disturbed you.

HORTON That is quite all right, my Lady. *(He puts the cushion centre of the settee.)* I realize that this is an exceptional evening. *(crossing to the door left)* Should you want me I shall be outside in the hall.

He exits.

MULVANEY *(heartily)* Well, Frenchy! How you been?

ELIZABETH *sits in the chair left centre.*

COLBERT *(right centre)* Very well, thank you. And you?

MULVANEY Oh, we've had a wonderful time, haven't we, Liz?

ELIZABETH Wonderful, Joe.

COLBERT You have been in the park?

MULVANEY Sure. How did you guess?

ELIZABETH It's the most heavenly night. There's a glorious full moon.

MULVANEY The searchlights made a swell background.

COLBERT I know.

MULVANEY *(to COLBERT)* Look, pal, do you mind fading away for a second? I've got a few things I still want to say to Liz.

COLBERT Very well. *(He gazes at them, then sighs deeply and goes into the bedroom.)*

MULVANEY *(moving down left)* Well, Liz? *(He leans against the radiogram.)*

ELIZABETH *(on the arm of the chair left centre)* Well, Joe?

MULVANEY I guess this is where we say it.

ELIZABETH I guess it is.

MULVANEY Seems kinda crazy, doesn't it?

ELIZABETH Kinda crazy is an understatement for everything that's happened to me in this last twenty-four hours.

MULVANEY You're sure this is the way you want it?

ELIZABETH Yes, Joe, and so are you.

MULVANEY I don't know so much about that.

ELIZABETH *(smiling)* Dulcie to you.

MULVANEY She's a good girl, Liz. Maybe one of these days I'll tell her about you.

ELIZABETH I should be careful about that. You wouldn't want to spoil Anglo-American relations now, would you?

MULVANEY Aw, she'd understand. She ought to be darned grateful to you, anyway, all things considered.

ELIZABETH She ought, but I wonder if she would be?

MULVANEY Do you think Bobby should be grateful to *me?*

ELIZABETH Yes, he should. Of course he should. You've been the little stranger that brings the severed couple together.

MULVANEY You forget that when this little stranger appeared on the scene the couple wasn't severed anyway.

ELIZABETH Yes, we were, Joe – in a way. I wasn't sure about Bobby. I don't think he was sure about me. We'd have got married all right, but – well, with my urge to experiment, who knows what trouble there might have been later?

MULVANEY You don't think there'll be trouble now?

ELIZABETH *(smiling)* Not if you keep your promise, Joe, and go right out of my life for ever.

MULVANEY Aw hell, Liz, I'm safe. You should know that by now. How long did we sit on that park bench?

ELIZABETH Nearly four hours.

MULVANEY Well, in four hours did I once...?

ELIZABETH No, but you did an awful lot of arguing.

MULVANEY Arguing's nothing.

ELIZABETH That rather depends on one's opponent. *(rising)* No, Joe, I'm sorry. You're just a little too attractive to be what you call safe. *(She crosses centre.)* I'll prefer you as a sentimental but distant memory.

MULVANEY Well, I guess this is where we say it. *(He moves in left centre.)*

ELIZABETH Yes, this is where we say it. Goodbye, Joe.

MULVANEY Goodbye, Liz. *(He holds out his arms.)*

ELIZABETH No, Joe.

MULVANEY Aw, come on, Liz, you can't say goodbye for ever to a guy standing fifty feet away from him.

ELIZABETH Have you forgotten I'm getting married today?

MULVANEY What about yesterday morning, then?

ELIZABETH That was different. You thought I was a trollop.

MULVANEY What did you think I was?

ELIZABETH One day I'll write and tell you. *(She crosses to him, her hand extended.)* Now, I'll just say goodbye.

MULVANEY *takes her hand, pulls her to him and kisses her. At this moment* COLBERT *appears up centre* ELIZABETH *breaks away to right centre,* COLBERT *comes downstage between them.*

COLBERT *(to* MULVANEY*)* I am most sorry to interrupt, but the Duke is anxious to talk to you. He is in the bedroom.

MULVANEY Ok. Don't they ever knock on doors in France?

He goes into the bedroom.

ELIZABETH Is Daddy still here? I'd better see him too. *(She moves up left of the settee as if to go to the bedroom door.)*

COLBERT *(stopping her)* Wait an instant, Milady. I must say it – I shall say it. You are making a hideous, horrible mistake.

ELIZABETH *(startled)* What?

COLBERT Turn back while there is still time – turn back before you ruin yet two more lives...

ELIZABETH *(moving away down right)* Oh, go away, you silly little man.

COLBERT *(following her)* Silly little man I may be now, Milady, but the day will dawn when you will see me in a different light.

MULVANEY *appears in the bedroom doorway.*

What is this American to you? Nothing. No more than a single evening of voluptuousness...

MULVANEY *(coming down centre)* Oh, is that all he is?

ELIZABETH *(moving round the right end of the settee to centre)* Don't pay any attention to him, Joe. Rise above him.

MULVANEY I've got a better idea. *(He crosses to COLBERT, rolling up his sleeves as if for a fight.)* I'm going to make him rise above *me!*

The DUKE *enters from the bedroom.* COLBERT *sits in the chair right,* MULVANEY *stands in the window.*

DUKE I say, this is capital news. Capital.

ELIZABETH *goes to the* DUKE.

So you've come to your senses at last, have you, my dear? *(He kisses her affectionately.)* I never doubted it. I know you too well. Headstrong – like to kick over the traces once in a while, but no real harm done. Just like your mother. There never *was* any truth in that Charlie Babington story.

HARPENDEN *enters from the hall and goes left of the* DUKE.

Ah, Robert, my boy, let me be the first to congratulate you—

HARPENDEN *(bewildered)* Thank you, sir.

DUKE *(jovially)* You're a sly dog, Robert, I must say. How did you pull it off, eh? That's what I want to know.

HARPENDEN Well, it wasn't awfully difficult.

ELIZABETH Just a minute, Daddy, I don't think Bobby can possibly know what we're talking about. *(to MULVANEY)* Joe – you tell him, will you?

MULVANEY *(down right centre)* Ok. Bobby, Elizabeth has turned me down flat because she says she's now quite sure she's still in love with you.

HARPENDEN Oh.

ELIZABETH Darling, is that all you're going to say – just – oh?

DUKE Don't worry, old girl. That's all he ever says, whatever you tell him. Isn't that so, Robert, my boy?

HARPENDEN *(with a sickly smile)* Yes, sir.

DUKE Go on, Robert, you old stick... *(pushing him across to* **ELIZABETH***)* Just go ahead and tell her how happy...

MABEL *enters up left in the red pyjamas.*

MABEL *(entering)* Darling, you always give me these awful red pyjamas... *(She stops at the sight of* **ELIZABETH***.)*

DUKE *(outraged)* Mabs!

MABEL I know, don't tell me. Back to the kitchen!

She exits left.

ELIZABETH That was Miss Crum, wasn't it?

DUKE *(to down left uneasily)* Yes, dear. Little Mabs Crum – very decent sort—

ELIZABETH Oh!

DUKE Now you mustn't get hold of the wrong end of the stick, old girl. As a matter of fact Mabs has been nipping in and out of here all the evening, hasn't she, boys?

COLBERT Yes, Monsieur.

MULVANEY Sure has, Duke.

ELIZABETH Oh! *(She sits on the left arm of the settee.)*

DUKE *(testily)* Now don't you start saying "Oh"! *(moving in down left centre)* Look here, old girl, I've been in these chambers myself the whole evening. Surely that should reassure you, if nothing else, that there's been no hanky-panky.

ELIZABETH I suppose it should, but oddly enough it doesn't.

DUKE But, my dear, this is a lot of ridiculous moonshine. Mabs is a sweet little child and we're all very fond of her, but she means nothing in the world to Robert, does she, my boy?

HARPENDEN Yes, sir – or rather no, sir – I mean—

DUKE Well, go on, out with it. Does she or does she not?

HARPENDEN Well, the fact is, I've just asked her to marry me.

COLBERT *rises.* ELIZABETH *rises and faces* HARPENDEN.

DUKE You what?

COLBERT It is true, Monsieur. I heard him. I even, I am afraid, encouraged the match.

DUKE *(roaring)* Keep out of this, you damned interfering little jackanapes.

COLBERT *(interested)* Qu'est-ce que c'est jackanapes?

DUKE Qu'est-ce que c'est jackanapes? Tell him, someone, tell him!

HARPENDEN Imbecile.

DUKE You're a damned interfering little imbecile. Allez-vous en! Retournez au kitchen!

COLBERT *(crossing up to the door left, with a volley of French, ending:)* ...I shall wait in the hall...always la cuisine!

DUKE *(moving up left centre)* Now, Robert, what is all this? You must be out of your mind. You say you've asked Mabs Crum to marry you?

HARPENDEN Yes, sir.

DUKE But in God's name, why?

HARPENDEN *(forlornly)* Well, I thought it was rather a good idea.

DUKE A good idea. A good idea to marry Crum? A woman who's spent her whole life popping in and out of bed with every Tom, Dick and Harry...

ELIZABETH I thought you said she was such a sweet little child?

DUKE *(turning on her)* You keep out of this too, Elizabeth. This is a matter for men to handle. Now look here, Robert...

ELIZABETH *(crossing to the DUKE)* Oh, Daddy, there's no point in going on like this. Take me home, please.

DUKE In a minute.

ELIZABETH Now! *(to HARPENDEN)* You had a perfect right to do what you like, I suppose. After all, I did turn you down.

HARPENDEN Elizabeth, I...

ELIZABETH *(turning sharply away from him)* Come on, Daddy...

She goes up left and exits.

DUKE *(with dignity)* All right, my dear. *(going to the door left)* I'm sure I don't want to stay another minute in the house of a raving madman... *(a thought strikes him)* Oh, just a moment, my dear. *(He returns to HARPENDEN.)* About that money you owe me...

HARPENDEN What money?

DUKE The six hundred pounds...

HARPENDEN You mean the five hundred and ninety pounds ten shillings. Yes, Duke, what about it?

DUKE It might interest you to know, young man, that I intend to hand over your cheque, when you send it to me, to charity.

HARPENDEN The charity in question being Messrs. Macdougall and Steinbeck, I presume, sir?

DUKE *(going to the door left)* Oh no, I've had those two ruffians called up! *(He exits.)* Come, my dear...

MULVANEY *(coming down centre to HARPENDEN)* I didn't make love to her, you know.

HARPENDEN *(listlessly)* Didn't you? Why not?

MULVANEY She wouldn't let me. *(a pause)* Congratulations on getting yourself engaged again.

HARPENDEN Thank you. *(He pauses.)* You know, I'm going to murder that bloody little Colbert!

MULVANEY You and me, both, brother.

COLBERT can be heard singing in the hall; he comes in looking delighted with himself. HARPENDEN and MULVANEY swing round to face him, facing upstage. He stops singing as he sees them, and moves down left, yawning and stretching.

COLBERT Tiens! I see I am faced by the Anglo-Saxon bloc. *(yawns)* It has been a full night. I think, Milord Bobby, I shall avail myself of your kind invitation and stake my claim in your bed.

MULVANEY *(to HARPENDEN)* Is he sleeping in our bed?

HARPENDEN Yes, he is.

A thought seems to strike them simultaneously.

MULVANEY Hm.

HARPENDEN Hm.

Suddenly they move together to the bedroom door, and open it.

MULVANEY *(making an elaborate bow to COLBERT)* Après vous, Monsieur.

COLBERT hesitates for some time, then straightens his shoulders, sets his tie straight and says with a determined air:

COLBERT Vive la France.

He walks into the bedroom with the air of an aristocrat going to the guillotine. **HARPENDEN** *and* **MULVANEY** *follow him and close the door.*

Curtain.

Scene Two

Scene. The same.

Time. About 10 a.m. that morning.

At the rise of the curtain HORTON *enters from the hall carrying a large tray with breakfast for three. He lays it on the drinks table, knocks on the centre door, and goes into the bedroom. After a moment there is the sound of voices, the word "Scram" only being heard clearly.* HORTON *reappears, takes up the tray and is going off left, when the doorbell rings.*

DUKE *(offstage)* Good morning, Horton.

HORTON *(offstage)* Good morning, your Grace.

DUKE *(entering)* Pay my taxi, will you, I've no change.

HORTON *(offstage)* Yes, your Grace.

DUKE *(crossing to the window and looking out)* Another Yankee grabbing a taxi! *(He goes to the chair left centre and sits.)*

HORTON *enters.*

Is nobody awake yet?

HORTON *(moving down left of the armchair)* All three gentlemen were asleep, your Grace, when I went in just now. I shook the shoulder nearest to the wall, which I took to be his Lordship's, but which proved to belong to the American gentleman, who told me to scram, which I understood to mean that they had all passed a restless night, and did not wish to be disturbed, and did not require breakfast.

DUKE You've heard the news, I suppose, Horton?

HORTON About his Lordship's engagement to Miss Crum? Yes, your Grace. He told me last night. *(He shakes his head gloomily.)*

DUKE I agree with you, Horton, it's a shocking business. He seems absolutely set on it, I gather?

HORTON I did attempt to indicate my disapproval, your Grace, with one of my looks, but for once he seemed quite unshaken. He said it was the only way he could see to save himself from extinction in the post-war world.

DUKE Talking like Bevan. Must be clean off his rocker.

HORTON I fear so, your Grace.

DUKE Oh well, I suppose we must both make the best of a bad job. Where is Miss Crum?

HORTON In the kitchen, your Grace.

DUKE Yes, of course, she would be. What's she doing up there?

HORTON Having a cup of tea, I fancy, your Grace.

MABEL *comes in left, dressed with her coat and hat on.*

MABEL *(crossing to centre)* Hullo, Tibby, it was you at the door, was it?

HORTON *crosses up and exits left.*

DUKE Yes, Mabs. Good morning. I came round especially to see you.

MABEL Did you, Tibby? *(She pecks him, and sits on the right arm of the armchair.)* How sweet of you.

DUKE It's not sweet of me at all. I want to talk to you seriously on a most urgent matter.

MABEL All right then. Fire away.

A pause. The DUKE *rises, crosses right centre, looking awkward and embarrassed.*

Come on, come on, don't keep me in suspense.

DUKE *(turning)* Well, I hardly know how to begin. *(urgently)* Mabs – have you ever heard of Zippy-Snaps?

MABEL Yes, of course, Tibby. Don't you remember – you showed me one once. It didn't work.

DUKE Didn't it? Astonishing thing. Faulty zipper I suppose. Anyway, it's a wonderful invention, my dear, it'll revolutionize women's dresses. None of this tiresome zipping and unzipping. Just zip snap, and there you are, ready to go out. *(going to her)* By the way, before we go any further, let me be the first to congratulate you on your engagement to young Robert.

MABEL Oh! Did he tell you that?

DUKE Yes. Last night. As a matter of fact we had a few words on the subject, I'm afraid, because at first I naturally felt a bit let down – on my daughter's behalf, you know.

MABEL Yes, of course, Tibby.

DUKE *(crossing back to right centre)* Still, thinking things over this morning, I thought – these days – it's no use crying over spilt milk, and the best thing I could do would be to come round and congratulate you on what I am sure will be an excellent match. *(He has turned to face her.)*

MABEL Thank you so much.

DUKE He's a blithering young idiot, of course, in many ways, but that's beside the point. Anyway, my dear, I hope you'll both be very happy. *(crossing to centre)* Now – returning to Zippy-Snaps.

MABEL Tibby, I've no money at all.

DUKE *(sitting on the chair left centre, beside her)* I know you haven't, my dear. It's not your money we want, it's you!

MABEL *(startled)* Me?

DUKE Exactly. Zippy-Snaps will, as we develop, cater mainly for the feminine sex, and I, as Chairman of the Board of Directors, have always maintained that what the Board needs is new blood – and – if possible – new feminine blood.

MABEL *(incredulously, rising)* You want *me* on the Board of Directors?

DUKE We do, my dear. You are exactly the sort of Director – or rather Directress – that we require. A smart, young, enterprising girl, with a very well-developed business sense.

MABEL *(sitting again on the arm of the chair)* Yes, and I suppose the fact that I'm the future Countess of Harpenden has nothing to do with it?

DUKE Well, of course, it's no good trying to hoodwink you, I can see – that is, I admit, a consideration. A title – and that title especially – will look very well on the prospectus.

MABEL Supposing I wasn't going to marry Bobby, would you still want me?

DUKE *(soothingly)* Of course, my dear, of course. I've told you – it's your talent and business acumen we want. *(suspiciously)* But you *are* going to marry Bobby, aren't you?

MABEL Well, he asked me to and I said yes.

DUKE Capital. *(He rises, moves centre and turns.)* Well, now, the whole thing is fixed. I rang up my fellow director this morning, and he agreed with the project entirely. The Board, in fact, is unanimous. Well, what do you say?

MABEL All right, Tibby.

DUKE *(moving to her)* We'll get the whole thing signed, sealed and delivered. My word! *(patting her on the cheek)* Won't Robert be proud of his little Mabs when he finds out what's happened to her. *(moving back to centre)* Let me see now – is there a typewriter here?

MABEL I don't think so, why?

DUKE I thought I'd just type out a couple of letters – perfectly legal – one from me to you – the other from you to me. Then we each sign them and the thing's done. *(calling off)* Horton! Horton!

MABEL By the way, Tibby, who's your fellow director?

DUKE Lord Finchingfield.

MABEL What? Not poor old Finchy? Is he out again?

DUKE *(mumbling, unable to look at her)* Oh, must you bring that up... So long ago.

HORTON enters up left.

HORTON Yes, your Grace?

DUKE Oh, Horton, does his Lordship keep a typewriter in his chambers?

HORTON No, your Grace, but I do.

DUKE Where is it?

HORTON Up in the kitchen, your Grace.

DUKE Lead me to it then, Horton. Don't go away now, Mabs, I'll be back in a jiffy.

He exits left, followed by **HORTON**. **MABEL**, *left alone, goes to the radiogram and switches it on. She then moves across to the window. The music blares forth, full up. After a moment* **MULVANEY** *enters from the bedroom, still almost asleep, goes to the radiogram, turns it off, then gropes his way back to bed. The doorbell rings.* **MABEL** *crosses up to the door left.*

MABEL *(calling)* It's all right, Horton, I'll answer it.

She exits. After a slight pause, she returns with **ELIZABETH**, *who enters first and crosses down right, leaving her hat and gloves on the telephone table.*

I thought it was you. *(moving down left)* Couldn't you get here any sooner?

ELIZABETH I came as quickly as I could. I had to finish my packing.

MABEL *(shutting the radiogram, and crossing to* **ELIZABETH***)* I'm glad you've come, anyway. You were so rude to me on the phone I thought you wouldn't. Won't you sit down?

ELIZABETH *(sitting at the right end of the settee)* Do you mind saying what you have to say fairly quickly as I have to catch a train at ten-forty-five?

MABEL *(looking at her watch)* I won't keep you more than five minutes. Bobby told you he'd asked me to marry him, didn't he?

ELIZABETH Yes, he did.

MABEL Did he tell you that I'd accepted him?

ELIZABETH No, but he hardly needed to tell me that.

MABEL Well, I did accept him, anyway, and do you know why?

ELIZABETH *(with a faint smile)* I think I can guess.

MABEL I doubt very much if you can. Because I'm very fond of him, and because I thought I'd make him a good wife.

ELIZABETH *(politely)* Really?

MABEL *(going to the telephone table, and getting a cigarette)* Yes. You see, I think he needs someone to take care of him, and I thought I'd be able to do that very well. *(She taps the cigarette.)*

ELIZABETH I agree that you've never seemed to find much trouble in taking care of yourself.

MABEL Yes. Unlike you, I've always had to, you see.

ELIZABETH You've managed very well.

MABEL Thank you. *(lighting the cigarette)* I haven't done too badly for myself, I must say.

ELIZABETH To be the Countess of Harpenden is quite an achievement.

MABEL *(regretfully – putting down the match)* Yes... Yes, it would have been, I suppose.

ELIZABETH Why "it would have been"?

MABEL Oh, because I'm not going through with it. That's what I wanted to tell you.

ELIZABETH Are you serious?

MABEL Perfectly. I told you I was very fond of Bobby. That's why I can't marry him. Does that make sense?

ELIZABETH No, it doesn't.

MABEL It does, really, if you think it out. *(She crosses to the settee, and sits at the left end.)* Now look, ducky – sorry – Lady Elizabeth – you can't imagine anyone behaving as badly – from your standards – as I do without, well, financial considerations being involved, can you? Oh hell, this polite beating about the bush gets me down. What I'm saying is, I am a trollop, let's face it, but not for money.

ELIZABETH What for then?

MABEL Men.

ELIZABETH Oh.

MABEL Now last night, up in the kitchen, I told Bobby that if I married him I'd stay faithful to him, and I meant it. But this morning, in the cold clear light of dawn, I just knew I couldn't go through with it.

ELIZABETH Perhaps, if you tried very hard...

MABEL No, it wouldn't matter how hard I tried. I can't lie to Bobby. So, regretfully, but firmly, I've got to turn him down – which, with two million and a title involved, is really quite something, don't you agree?

ELIZABETH It *is* quite something, I do agree. I must say I'm surprised.

MABEL My dear, *I'm* amazed. But there it is. He's too sweet and he's too easy to cheat. So I can't do it. Of course with an old idiot like Tibby...

ELIZABETH You mean my father?

MABEL Sorry, dear, I forgot he was your father. *(She looks at ELIZABETH.)* I must say you'd never think it. Well, there you are, Elizabeth, I'm throwing your earl back in your face. Do you still want him?

ELIZABETH I don't know.

MABEL He still wants you.

ELIZABETH *(pointing to the bedroom)* Is Bobby in there?

MABEL Oh yes, all the Allies are in there.

ELIZABETH Do you think you could get him out without waking the others?

MABEL I'll try, but it won't be easy. *(She rises, goes towards the bedroom door, and turns.)* By the way, if you're getting married this morning, it's very unlucky to see him.

ELIZABETH *(rising startled)* Married this morning?

MABEL *(coming down to her)* Why, have you put off all the guests?

ELIZABETH No, we didn't have time. They're going to make an announcement.

MABEL Well, that's fine. If you hurry you can still make it. It'd be a pity to disappoint all the guests.

ELIZABETH Yes. But – but – I don't know. Well, anyway I must see him first.

MABEL All right, Auntie Mabel will fix it. Now you stand there, *(She moves* ELIZABETH *to beside the phone table, her back to the door up centre.)* so that you can't see the door, and I'll do the rest.

She disappears into the bedroom and emerges after a few moments with a tousled, sleepy, disgruntled-looking HARPENDEN, *who is walking with his eyes closed. He has on his sailor trousers and vest.*

HARPENDEN *(plaintively)* But why have I got to keep my eyes closed? Please may I go back to bed? What is this?

MABEL *(moving him till he stands with his back to* ELIZABETH, *facing the window)* I'll tell you all about it in a minute. There! Now you can open your eyes.

HARPENDEN *opens his eyes, blinking in the sunlight.*

But don't look round. Look straight ahead. *(She collects her gloves off the table behind the settee.)*

HARPENDEN All right, I am looking. *(wearily)* What's it going to be? A lovely choc for baby?

MABEL Yes, darling. A lovely choc for baby. I'm not going to marry you.

HARPENDEN *(eagerly)* Aren't you? *(discarding his obvious delight)* Aren't you, Mabel? Why?

MABEL There really isn't time to go into that – just now. Let's just say that I don't approve of marriage as an institution.

HARPENDEN Do you really mean you're turning me down?

MABEL Flat.

HARPENDEN Oh! I'm very upset.

MABEL You know, darling, that would have much more conviction if you could get rid of that joyous gleam in your eye. *(She kisses him.)* Goodbye. Bobby, how much do you love Elizabeth?

HARPENDEN Very much.

MABEL That's what I thought. *(crossing down left)* Don't you dare look round. *(going to the door left)* For the very last time in my life I am going up to your kitchen.

She exits.

ELIZABETH Bobby?

HARPENDEN *(without turning)* Yes, Elizabeth?

ELIZABETH You knew I was here?

HARPENDEN I guessed it.

ELIZABETH Is that why you said you were very much in love with me?

HARPENDEN No. That's the truth.

ELIZABETH Do you know why we mustn't look at each other this morning?

HARPENDEN I guessed that too.

ELIZABETH Do you still want to marry me, darling?

HARPENDEN More than anything on earth.

ELIZABETH In spite of everything that's happened?

HARPENDEN If you still want to marry me, that's good enough.

ELIZABETH I do still want to marry you. More now than ever before.

HARPENDEN In spite of having no white-hot burning thing-ammy for me?

ELIZABETH White-hot burning thingammy's a mistake. It may be all right for some people – but not for me.

HARPENDEN I think I ought to warn you that I'm a doomed man.

ELIZABETH Doomed, darling? To what?

HARPENDEN Extinction, I think.

ELIZABETH I don't care, provided we both get extinguished together.

HARPENDEN That's by far the nicest thing you've ever said to me.

ELIZABETH I can think of a nicer thing I might say. It's true too.

HARPENDEN What's that?

ELIZABETH I'm in love with you, Bobby.

HARPENDEN Yes. That's even nicer.

ELIZABETH (picking up her hat and gloves from the phone table, and going to the door left) Don't look round. I'll see you in five minutes' time – in church. Goodbye.

HARPENDEN Goodbye.

ELIZABETH goes out. HARPENDEN stands stock still for a moment, then suddenly comes to life, dashes to the bedroom door and opens it.

(shouting) Hey, you two. Wake up! Help me dress! I'm getting married! *(bushing to the hall door)* Horton, bring my boots down! Iron my collar! And step on it, for God's sake!

COLBERT and MULVANEY come out of the bedroom. They wear a pair of pyjamas between them, COLBERT has the top half. They go to the settee, COLBERT sits centre, MULVANEY on the arm left, HARPENDEN goes to the telephone, feeling his beard.

MULVANEY What's all the noise about?

HARPENDEN *(dialling)* I'm getting married.

MULVANEY Yeah, I know.

HARPENDEN You don't know. You can't possibly know. *(into the phone)* Hullo, Boots? ...This is Lord Harpenden. I want a new razor blade...but you must have – I'm getting married ! Oh, all right. *(He rings off.)*

HORTON *(entering, carrying a sailor collar)* I've had no time to iron your collar, my Lord. Is it very urgent?

HARPENDEN Of course it's very urgent. I'm getting married in five minutes. Hell, no, three minutes. Oh God, I suppose I can always say I'm growing a beard. *(He dashes into the bedroom.)*

HORTON Who is his Lordship marrying in three minutes?

MULVANEY Search me!

HARPENDEN appears again, trying to put on his collar. He goes to MULVANEY, who ties it for him.

HARPENDEN Hey, Joe, does one get married in a gas mask?

MULVANEY *(tying strings of the collar behind him)* It depends who you're marrying, brother!

HARPENDEN Idiot! I meant, does one carry a gas mask – full-dress and all that? Do you know, Horton?

HORTON I fancy not, my Lord. I am not sure if the rule applies to ratings, of coarse, but my brother, who is a lieutenant-commander, did not carry his at his wedding.

HARPENDEN All right, Horton. Jump to it, man, for heaven's sake. *(He moves up to the door centre.)*

MULVANEY *(following him)* Hey, wait a minute. He wants to know who you're marrying, and so do we.

HARPENDEN Oh, didn't I tell you? Elizabeth.

HORTON I am most relieved, my Lord. You'll be leaving for Oxford after the wedding?

HARPENDEN Yes, Horton.

HORTON Very good, my lord.

He exits left.

MULVANEY *(left of* HARPENDEN*)* Gee, Bobby, I don't know what to say.

HARPENDEN I'll take it as said. *(They shake hands).* Thanks, Joe.

COLBERT *(rising and moving to right of* HARPENDEN*)* I, on the other hand, *do* know what to say. England has once again muddled through!

The DUKE*'s voice and* MABEL*'s can be heard in the hall.*

HARPENDEN Quick, into the bedroom, both of you. If you're coming to the wedding, you've got to get dressed.

He pushes COLBERT *and* MULVANEY *into the bedroom.* COLBERT *pulls the curtains open.* MABEL *and the* DUKE *come in, each carrying a typed letter.*

Hullo, sir. See you in church.

He exits to the bedroom.

DUKE *(centre of the double doors)* See me in church? Now what the dickens does he mean by that?

MABEL *(crossing the desk)* I've no idea, Tibby.

DUKE See me in church? Has the boy gone off his rocker?

MABEL *(at the desk)* Yes, ducky, I expect so. Where do I sign?

DUKE At the bottom.

> **HORTON** *enters left, carrying a pair of boots. He dashes round the* **DUKE** *and into the bedroom.*

God bless my soul! What on earth's the matter with Horton?

MABEL Darling, I don't know.

> **HORTON** *repeats the performance, coming from the bedroom, round right of the* **DUKE.**

HORTON *(breathless)* I beg your pardon, your Grace.

He exits left.

DUKE Has Horton gone cuckoo too?

> *He goes to the desk to sign the letter. As he picks up the pen* **MULVANEY** *dashes in from the bedroom, and goes to the desk opening and shutting drawers violently, ignoring the* **DUKE.**

MULVANEY *(pushing the* **DUKE** *aside)* Pardon me, Duke – *(calling)* Hey, Bobby, which drawer is that ring in?

HARPENDEN *(offstage)* Right-hand top.

MULVANEY *(pushing past the* **DUKE** *again and opening the top right-hand drawer)* Ok, I got it. Thanks, Duke. *(He darts back into the bedroom, carrying a small ring-box.)*

DUKE *(roaring)* Has everyone gone raving mad in this house this morning?

MABEL *(putting a pen in his hand)* Go on, Tibby dear, I'm late for the office already.

DUKE I've done it.

HARPENDEN *comes in, dressed but with his collar inside his sailor blouse. He goes down left to the mirror.*

HARPENDEN Darling, smooth my collar.

MABEL *(going to him, and setting the collar to rights)* There you are. Bobby, isn't it lovely? I've just been made a director of Zippy-Snaps.

HARPENDEN Have you, darling. Aren't you a clever girl?

MABEL I've had the most wonderful time, what with your two thousand and being made a director...

DUKE *(coming right of the settee to below it – chuckling)* Two thousand, eh? That's a neat little engagement present, I must say.

HARPENDEN What does he mean?

MABEL I don't know, darling. I think he's a bit batty this morning. Goodbye, Bobby.

HARPENDEN Aren't you coming?

MABEL No, I've got to go to work.

HARPENDEN Goodbye, then, darling. *(He kisses her.)* You've been an angel.

MABEL Not really. I'd have made an awful muck of it, I know.

HARPENDEN I wish you were coming to the church.

MABEL Better not. I might suddenly change my mind. Goodbye, Bobby dear. *(She goes to the door, and looks back at the DUKE.)* Goodbye, Tibby darling, see you on the Board!

She exits.

DUKE (*moving towards* HARPENDEN) Why do you wish she were coming to the church? Why did you say you'd see me in church? What is all this church nonsense?

HARPENDEN (*centre*) My God, don't you know?

DUKE Know? Know what?

HARPENDEN I'm marrying your daughter.

DUKE Good God! When?

HARPENDEN (*looking at his watch*) Two minutes ago.

The DUKE *stares at* HARPENDEN *for a second, and at the letter in his hand, then makes a dash for the hall door.*

DUKE Hey, Mabs! Mabs! Wait a minute! I want to see you – Mabs!

He is off before the end of the speech. MULVANEY *and* COLBERT *come out of the bedroom, dressed, both make a dive for* HARPENDEN.

MULVANEY Say, listen, Bobby, I'm to be best man, aren't I?

COLBERT On the contrary, he agreed that it was I who had the first claim.

MULVANEY (*hotly*) First claim nothing! After doing your level best to gum up the entire works!

COLBERT I to gum up the works? Who was it who rendered the bride insensible from drink?

MULVANEY Say, listen, there's only one way to settle this. (*He brings out the craps from his pocket.*) The fair play!

They both kneel on the floor centre, facing each other. HARPENDEN *between them standing. As they flip the dice, the* DUKE *comes back, breathless.*

HARPENDEN (*crossing down left to the* DUKE) Did you catch her?

DUKE Afraid not. But she caught *me* all right, the little scallywag.

HARPENDEN I won't hear a word against Mabel Crum.

DUKE Mabel Crum. What a name on a prospectus!

HARPENDEN Yes.

MULVANEY (chanting, on the floor) Little four, hit that floor.

DUKE (crossing centre of them) Hullo! What's going on here?

HARPENDEN They're playing to see who's going to be best man.

DUKE God bless my soul! What next?

MULVANEY (chanting) Come up for Daddy! This baby wants to be best man!

COLBERT This baby wants to be best man!

DUKE Which do you fancy – France or America?

HARPENDEN I don't mind.

DUKE Well, you take America, I'll take France.

HARPENDEN All right.

DUKE Five hundred?

HARPENDEN Right. Five hundred.

DUKE Done. Monsieur, I've put a monkey on you! (putting his hand on **COLBERT**'s shoulder)

COLBERT (leaning back in amazement) Comment?

DUKE J'ai mette un singe sur vous! Play up! Play up!

The others join in, cheering as—

The curtain falls.

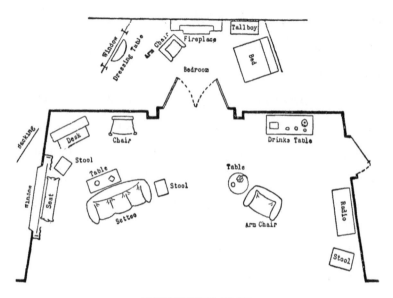

FURNITURE PLOT

O.P.

On wall. 2 pictures.
Downstage Right. Underneath. Ladder-back chair
Right – Window. Brocade curtains and pelmet.
  Net curtains.
  Outside window. Window-box and flowers.
  Underneath. Duet stool.
Upstage Right. Bureau bookcase.
  On desk. Blotter.
    Inkstand.
    Pen tray and pens.
    Clock.
    Silver candlestick.
    Cigarette box.
    Glass ashtray.
    Papers in pigeon holes.
  In right-hand drawer. Cheque.
    Ring box.

In bookcase. Books.
    Bottle of whisky.
    Bottle of gin.
Back Wall. On wall. 2 pictures.
  Right. Underneath. Ladder-back chair.
  Centre. Double doors.
  Left. On wall. 3 pictures.
    Underneath. Large polished table.
      On it. Tray with 6 glasses, water jug. Decanter.
      Syphon in silver holder. Table lamp. Ashtray
      with match box. Cigarette box. Magazines. New
      Statesman.

P.S.

Upstage Left. Hall door.
  On wall. Empire mirror.
    Electric wall brackets.
  Underneath. Radiogram with bowl of roses on it.
    Glass ashtray.
Downstage Left. Brocade-covered stool.
Left centre. Armchair with brocade cushion.
Right centre. Of armchair. Small table.
  On it. Telephone.
    Cigarette box.
    Glass ashtray.
    Silver matchbox.
Right centre – Settee with 2 covered brocade cushions and 1
    brown on centre.
Left centre. Of settee. Brocade-covered stool.
Behind settee. Table.
  On it. Table lamp.
    Bowl of flowers.
    3 books.
    Ashtray.
    Silver matchbox.
    Cigarette box.

Bedroom Upstage Centre
(Seen through double doors.)

Right. Window. Curtain.

Venetian blind.

Back wall. Large mirror.

Underneath it. Dressing table.

On it. Travelling toilet set.

Hairbrushes.

Framed photo.

Bottle of lotion, etc.

Centre back wall. Large print.

Underneath. 2 miniatures.

Underneath. Mantelshelf.

On it. 2 framed photos.

Pair of candlesticks.

Gilt clock.

On floor. Hearth rug.

Upstage Left. On wall. 3 small prints.

Underneath. Tallboy.

On it. Pair of bookends.

Books.

Silver photo frame.

Left centre. Double divan bed.

On it. Eiderdown.

Blanket.

P.S. Off. *On wall.* Print.

Underneath. Wooden hall chair.

PROPERTY PLOT (STAGE AND PERSONAL)
ACT I

Offstage Left. 2 breakfast trays (**HORTON**).
On each. Cup and saucer.
Plate and sausage.
Silver dish-cover.
Coffee pot.
Toast rack.
Napkin.
2 knives.
1 fork.
1 teaspoon.
Small plate.
Tray cloth.
Times on tray for **HARPENDEN**.
MULVANEY's uniform.
HARPENDEN's sailor hat and boots.
In Bedboom. Dressing gown (**MULVANEY**).
Eiderdown (**MULVANEY**).
Onstage. *On telephone table.* Paper (**HARPENDEN**).
On settee table. Wallet (**HARPENDEN**).
On bookcase upstage right. Bottle of whisky (**MULVANEY**).

After ACT I

All ashtrays cleaned.
All dirty glasses replaced.
Cushions on settee and chair tidied. Curtains closed.

ACT II

Cheque in right-hand drawer of bureau.
On table left centre – 1 glass of gin, and 1 glass of whisky, for
    CRUM and **MULVANEY**.
On table upstage left – 4 glasses.
    Bottle of gin *(right)*.
    Bottle of whisky *(left)*.

On table upstage right – Book for **HARPENDEN**.
Brocade-stool down stage left *is struck*.
Offstage. 2 dice (**MULVANEY**).
    Latch keys (**HARPENDEN**).
    Hat (**COLBERT**).

After ACT II

All ashtrays cleaned.
All dirty glasses replaced by clean ones on tray.
Cushions on settee and chair tidied up.
Curtains remain closed.
In right-hand drawer of desk is ring box.
Centre cushion on settee goes on floor downstage end of settee
           with a glass of whisky on each side, and paper
           and pencil right **DUKE** and **HARPENDEN**.
On table upstage left – 4 glasses.
    Bottle of gin left (Note change.)
    Bottle of whisky right (Note change).
Brocade-stool from right centre to down stage left.
Offstage. Red pyjamas (**MABEL**).
    Travelling rug (**HORTON**).
    Breakfast set for three (**HORTON**).
    2 typed letters (**DUKE** and **MABEL**).
For Scene Two. *During quick change.* Curtains opened. Ashtrays
        cleaned.
    Dirty glasses replaced by clean ones.
    Cushions tidied.

Offstage Effects

ACT I. Telephone bell.
    Front-doorbell.
    Radiogram playing.
ACT II. Front-doorbell. Act HI.
    Scene One. Nothing.
    Scene Two. Front-doorbell.
        Radio playing.

LIGHTING PLOT USED AT
THE GLOBE THEATRE, LONDON

Electrics Layout for Batten, Floats, Spots, etc.

No. 1 Batten. 3 straw, 36 pink, 52 pale gold.

Floats. Frosted 36 pink, frosted 52 gold, Open white.

Spot Bar.	No.	1.	36.	No.	7.	3 and F.
	No.	2.	7.	No.	8.	3.
	No.	3.	3.	No.	9.	3.
	No.	4.	36.	No.	10.	3.
	No.	5.	3 and F.	No.	11.	3.
	No.	6.	3 and F.	No.	12.	Open white.

Upstage Spot Bar.—No.	1.	4.	P.S.
No.	2.	7.	
No.	3.	3.	
No.	4.	Open white O.P.	

Stage Floods, P.S. 500 Watt. Flood. 3 and F. ACT I and ACT III, Scene Two. 4 and F. ACT II and ACT III, Scene One.

O.P. *Down Stage.*	Flood No.	1.	17.
	Flood No.	2.	Open white.
	Flood No.	3.	Open white.
	Flood No.	4.	Open white.
	Mirror No.	5.	Open white.
	Pageant No.	6.	Open white.
	Pageant No.	7.	Open white.
	Pageant No.	8.	Open white.

O.P. *Upstage.*	Flood No.	9.	Open white.
	Flood No.	10.	Open white.

Two table lamps. Right centre and upstage left with amber lamps.

Perches. 3 aside, frosted 3.

F.O.H. 4 frosted 51.

Offstage Spots and Floods and Spot Bab Positions

Spot Bar.	No.	1.	Upstage centre, chair left to centre doors.
	No.	2.	Round chair left.
	No.	3.	Upstage end of settee right.

No. 4. Downstage end of settee right.

No. 5. Upstage left chair left to hall door to lamp upstage left.

No. 6. On centre doors.

No. 7. Upstage right behind settee right to desk.

No. 8. On centre settee right.

No. 9. On chair left.

No. 10. Upstage end settee right to cover stool right centre.

No. 11. Downstage centre to front of chair left.

No. 12. Downstage centre in front of chair left and settee right.

Upstage Spot Bar. No. 1. Middle of bed and to centre.

No. 2. End of bed and to centre.

No. 3. Overlap on No. 2 to right centre.

No. 4. Overlap on No. 3 to window.

F.O.H. No. 1. Down right to right centre

No. 2. Right centre to centre.

No. 3. Centre to left centre.

No. 4. Left centre to down left.

Perches. P.S. No. 1. Settee right.

No. 2. Down centre to settee.

No. 3. Chair left.

O.P.No. 1. Down left centre.

No. 2. Chair left.

No. 3. Settee and right centre.

Offstage Lighting. P.S. Flood through hall door.

O.P. Flood No. 1. On to top of backing.

Spot No. 2. On to flowers in window-box.

Downstage. Flood No. 3. On stage half of backing.

Flood No. 4. Off stage half of backing.

Mirror No. 5. On doors centre.

Pageant No. 6. On hall door left.

Pageant No. 7. Flood through window.
Pageant No. 8. On chair left.

Upstage. Flood No. 9. Through bedroom window on wall.

          Flood No. 10. Through bedroom window on wall.

LIGHTING PLOT

ACT I

No. 1 *Batten.* 36 and 3 full.
Floats. Open white, 36, 52 full.
F.O.H. Nos. 1–4 full.
Perches. Nos. 1–3 on O.P. and P.S. full.
Spots. Nos. 1, 3, 5, 6, 7, 8, 9, 10, 11, 12 full.
    Nos. 2 and 4 at ¾.
O.P. *and* P.S. All stage dips with pageants, floods, etc., full.
At cue. Upstage spot bar Nos. 2, 3, 4 full.

ACT II

No. 1 *Batten.* 36 and 52 at ¼.
Floats. Open white, 36 at ¼.
F.O.H. Full.
Perches. Full.
Spots. 1 to 12 full.
P.S. Stage dips full.
Two table lamps and wall brackets alight.
Upstage spot bar Nos. 1 and 2 at full.
At cue. Centre section floats 36. Open white to full.

ACT III

Scene One. Same as ACT II. (Without cue.)
Scene Two. Same as ACT I. (With light cue.)

SIMPLIFIED LIGHTING PLOT

ACT I

Floats. Amber, pink, and white, all full.

No. 1 Batten. Amber, pink, and white, full.

No. 2 Batten. Amber and pink, full. White, ½.

No. 3 Batten (over bedroom). Amber and pink, ¼. White, nil.

F.O.H. No. 51 frosted.

Perches. No. 3 straw, frosted, P.S. on settee and armchair. O.P. on settee, armchair, and down left centre. *Amber lengths on interior backing left.*

Flood exterior cloth O.P. Top half No. 17 blue. Stage half, open white.

Stage floods white and straw through window.

White flood through bedroom window on cue. (Curtains drawn open.)

ACT II

To Open. Floats.—White and pink, ¼.

No. 1 Batten. Amber and pink, ¾.

No. 2 Batten. Amber and pink O.P. and centre sections, ¼. P.S. section full.

F.O.H. No. 51 frosted.

Perches. As for ACT I.

Interior backing, as for ACT I.

Exterior backing, nil. *(Curtains drawn.)*

Table lamps and wall brackets on.

Cue. Bring up centre section of floats, pink and white, for crap game, slowly as business starts.

ACT III

Scene One. As for ACT I. (Without cue.)

Scene Two. As for ACT II. (With light cue.)

VISIT THE SAMUEL FRENCH BOOKSHOP AT THE ROYAL COURT THEATRE

Browse plays and theatre books, get expert advice and enjoy a coffee

Samuel French Bookshop
Royal Court Theatre
Sloane Square
London
SW1W 8AS
020 7565 5024

Shop from thousands of titles on our website

 samuelfrench.co.uk

 samuelfrenchltd

 samuel french uk

Lightning Source UK Ltd.
Milton Keynes UK
UKHW020638151121
393997UK00009B/373

9 780573 014802